GOD'S LOVE

Barry Gaddis

WESTBOW
PRESS®
A DIVISION OF THOMAS NELSON
& ZONDERVAN

WestBow Press books may be ordered through booksellers or by contacting:

WestBow Press
A Division of Thomas Nelson & Zondervan
1663 Liberty Drive
Bloomington, IN 47403
www.westbowpress.com
1 (866) 928-1240

ISBN: 978-1-9736-7514-3 (sc)
ISBN: 978-1-9736-7513-6 (e)

Print information available on the last page.

WestBow Press rev. date: 09/19/2019

Contents

Here I am lost in the darkness.
Drained of all life and happiness.
So far down the sun cannot find.
Trapped in a prison of my mind.
I met a man playing songs from a Christian band.
To my surprise he was sent from a far away land.
I listened to what he had to say.
Things of happiness love and a new way.
I was so tired of my wicked boss.
Gave my life to a man hanging on a cross
He took away my guilt and shame.
And the life of the devils game.
He gave me a gift of heavens key.
The Holy Spirit running wild inside of me.
Now you see this one I love.
Who came to me swiftly like a dove.
Please come to Jesus and understand.
God is always by your side with a helping hand.

To Brittany:
God put you in my life for a reason.Your heart is the most pure
and beautiful that I have ever known. I thank God every day
for sending such a beautiful Angel, to touch and bless my life.
Thank you for being you.
And your help with this book.
You are truly a blessing from God.
Please believe these few words;
To truly believe and understand It's not about saving everyone.

Because I can't save everyone.
It's about saving that one.
The very special one in his eye.

This is why I'm here!!!

(you)

I have a special thanks to Pastor Bill For allowing God to work through him. To get my head thinking "the right way."

THANK YOU!!

I have a very special thank you. To my beautiful niece Trinity. For all your help with editing this book. You are definitely the one God chose.

Thank you Trinity – "I love you"

Introduction

God just hit me with something. He's telling me I need to listen to what I'm writing, that a lot of the things he says are to help me too. I need to accept what is going through me. Yes, I can admit that I just let it come in and go out, not stopping to think about what is really being said. So now I'm going to have to let his words stop in my head until I truly understand what he is saying. Then I can put them down in writing. I really did think that I was doing his work by writing his words. I never thought that he meant them for me too. Now he is saying, "Why do you not listen to me?". Ok, God I'm all yours! You do so much for me. You show me things and teach me every day. I really did believe I was doing everything you wanted. I always did read what I wrote to really listen to your words. I see what you are saying now. Writing and reading doesn't mean I'm listening. It's amazing how you do this to me. You give me words that I never thought about. Now your telling me to think about everything you say to me. I do know there's so much to be learned in your words.

Ok, what are we going to talk about now? How about the way people think that they're "good" with God. They make the same mistake I just made, not listening to you. They believe that they are "good" with you. Maybe because they go to church on Sunday. Maybe because they are saved. Or even because they gave their life to you. Just doing those things don't make you "good" with God. You really do have to have a relationship with God, Jesus, and the

Holy Spirit. That is how my relationship is with you. You're my everything. Nothing could ever take me away from you.

Thank you for being so good to me. The things you do for me never stop. To look at where I was years ago and compare that to where I'm at today. It's a big change for real. I'm so happy I found my way to you. Thank you for sending pastor Bill, and Brittany to be a part of my life. You always know what to do and who to send. Thank you for everything you do. Not just for me for everyone. Please just keep working in others' lives. The way you work in mine. I have seen your hand at work. It is the most amazing thing to be able to see you work in every life. I'm watching you work in a life that is special to me. It's so awesome the way you change the way people think. I will forever praise you every day.

Thank you lord!!

My Testimony.....

I'm going to start this story by telling you about a childhood of abuse where your reality mixes with dark dreams. You go through so much anger and disbelief. Life is full of pain and emotional hatred until you start wondering.

Then, you start asking yourself over and over why you were even born. Were you born to be tortured and abused. When you're a kid you can't answer yourself, so you withdraw into yourself until the day when something wakes you up.

Unfortunately for me, that was the day I was turned on to weed. That was a life changer, especially after I started selling. I went from being a nobody to being everybody's friend.

Everything that came with this weed seemed really good to me at that time. Money, friends, and girls! What else did I need?! That's when I started looking for a better high. I went to drinking, then to the pills.

I did a lot of stupid stuff back then. I learned at a young age that girls will do anything for what they want, so I used them. That caused me to lose respect and trust for all women. I was a drug addict with a lot of issues, so I started trying other drugs like acid speed. Well, anything that was around. Then, one day at a party, I meet this girl. I started hanging out partying. She was pregnant, so I took her in. I cared for her and the baby. I ended up marrying her. The partying never stopped. Five years later, she had my son.

This is where life went downhill with no breaks. My son was born blind. This was the first and only time I asked God for something in that life, but you know what, I never believed in him. I didn't know him. I never looked at what was done for my son at that time. He had six surgeries on his eyes before he was one year old. He can see a little out of one eye. The other, not a thing. At that'll point, there was no God to me. I fell really hard.

While my son was going through operations, I had an accident at work and crushed my feet. The drugs they gave me overtook everything. I lost so much time and memory here. I can remember going to a bar drinking and eating pills. I don't remember leaving.

I woke up with my car on the side of a mountain. The motor was in the driver's seat, and I was laying in the back. I tried to move, but the pain overtook me. When I came to, I pulled myself out of the window. I could not use my feet or legs. I hit the ground and passed out again. I had a broken back and was air cared to the hospital. They gave me more drugs on top of what I had for my feet.

I laid in bed doped up big time for months, until one day, no one was around. I had to go really bad!! I rolled over, put my feet on the floor, and stood up holding on to things. I made it in the bathroom.

Over the next month, I worked on walking. Then I was off again. This time I had really good drugs. While I was out doing stupid stuff, I ended up in a fight with the police. I went straight to jail. Did not pass go, did not collect 200. I was sent to the pen. There were no drugs in the pen, or so I thought. I found this thing called heroin. I thought I was in heaven. See how the enemy lies to us?

To sum it all up, my life was over at that point. I had found the high that I was looking for. Just put it in a needle and done. I thought I had found the ultimate high, until one day, some girl said lets put coke in it. Wow. Instantly dead man walking.

It's amazing what the enemy will do to keep you in his hands. I ended up in and out of jails, rehabs, and yes, the pen 2 more times. I was so gone and didn't even know it. I was the devil's best friend. I knew that I was a condemned man. I kept telling myself that I was an addict. I was living as an addict and I would die an addict. Nothing could ever change that. Believe me, I tried enough times.

Then came the day that I was trying to get the warrants off me. I went to turn myself in on a needle charge. I forgot that I had a needle in my pocket. Now 2 charges. I got 90 days in jail. When I went back to court, the judge said that I could do 30 days in the casa program. No brainer take 30 days. Faster I can go back to doing what I have been doing.

When I got to the casa program, I was there for about 4 days. This guy came up to me and asked me if I wanted to go to celebrate recovery group. I asked what's that – he said it's like NA or AA, but If you don't go there, you will have to do yoga class. "I'm in". Never knew it at that time, but I made the choice that would change my life.

I met this man, Pastor Bill. I remember the first night. I sat in the back and listened to the music. Then I found myself wanting to go the second time. So I talked to Pastor Bill. We talked about me trying to kill myself with overdose. I told him how I would go lock myself in a room and do so much I shouldn't ever wake up. Every time EMS. waking me up. Once or twice I could see, but 4 times and every time a different place.

Pastor Bill just said to me. Think about who could put someone there every time. I went back to my bunk and thought about this for hours. I had a lot of things running through my head. I knew I was done just waiting to die.

I picked up my bible and opened it up what i saw was ASK, SEEK, KNOCK MATTHEW 7: 7 Ask and it will be given. Seek and you will find. Knock and the door will be opened.

Ok now how did I open to this? I'm starting to believe there is a God. A little faith. So I turned around and said let's try this. I have no other choice. It's this or death. I'm beyond done. Please, God I give all my life to you because if I have control of it, I'm dead. I just can't live anymore. My life is over. Please God help me. Take all this bad stuff away from me. Then I went to sleep.

When I woke up, my body felt so light. Hey, what is this a smile on my face, the happiness in me, the joy, the love in my heart. Wow, what happened to me "I'm changed". Then everything overwhelmed me at once.

I had to sit down. I just knew at that point that I would never have to live with the enemy again. Yes, I lived with him. I sat at his table and ate dinner with him, entertained him, done what he wanted me to do. I believed his lies. I really thought that life was the way to live. Now, God pulled me out of the deepest darkest pit in Satan's dungen. He did it so fast that all the bad stuff got left there with the old me.

I wanted to see Pastor Bill. I had to tell him. I walked in to CR and asked him to play the song changed by Rascal flatts for me. After group I walked up to him. He gave me a hug. I could tell he knew. When I got out of jail,there was not a thought of drinking or even drugs. But the first step out, I lit up a cigarette. Nasty. That was the last time. Yes, God took that from me too.

This is what I did to stay clean. Ok well, the first thing was that I gave my life to God. Let me tell you this first. I was so disgusted with who I had become. I for real gave up on life. I tried to kill myself by overdose. I didn't have any will to live anymore. Yes, I knew I was dead already. I was just waiting for the day that I would not be here anymore. All of that changed when God gave me a new life.

You see, I had a reason to live, a purpose in life again, a meaning. When I realized this, I really wanted this new life. I did everything different this time. I had to humble myself. I asked pastor Bill for help. This was new to me. I've never done anything like this before.

I had to understand that everything had to change. Not only was I going without drugs, I was giving up alcohol and cigarettes. That was a very big change. After a lifetime of doing these things. It's amazing how we let things control us. I never understood this until now.

Ok, I went without a phone for 3 months. When I did get my phone turned on, I deleted all of the numbers on it. I started completely over. I almost forgot to tell you this. I walked away from everything, my marriage, and everyone. Let me tell you something.

There were times when I would think about that life, but I knew that I didn't want it anymore.

See, I had money in my pocket. I knew that I could go out and get anything I wanted, but I didn't want any drugs. I wanted to live this new way. I walked to work until I got my license back. Then I bought a truck, but until then, I would get rides or walk to meetings. I went to NA or celebrate recovery every day. I never missed a meeting in 258 days.

I made new friends, people that were clean. With this came opportunities for new and better jobs. I worked very hard at staying clean. I knew that if I went back to that life, I would be dead.

All of the people that I met each taught me things. One big thing was helping other people. I learned that other people had troubles too. Some were worse than what I was going through, but for real the thing that made this worth everything to me was knowing that my past was gone. God forgave me for all I had done. Just having all that shame and guilt removed. It's amazing how that can change everything.

Yes I did have to work at this life. Without God I would never have been able to do it because to me, then, I was an addict. I was living as an addict, and I knew that I would die an addict. You see, that was my life then. So now do you understand? Yes, I did work at it only after God gave me new life a reason to live. I just stayed in my walk with God.

I'm not perfect. I'm still broken. Do I stumble? Yes. Do I fall? Yes sometimes I do, but I have God there helping me up. He's putting me back on my feet. Now, so much weight has been removed. I'm not looking at the ground anymore.

You know, I never had a life before God gave me new life. I never got to experience the joys of life. I only got to do the things that I thought were fun. That's because I was living with the devil. He wants us to live thinking his ways are fun, hoping we get stuck in his ways.

I realized the enemy never had to steal anything from me. I was weak. I gave him everything he wanted. That's exactly what he wanted. He wanted my eyes to be blinded to the truth. He wants us to think his way is where we find happiness. The bad thing is that we do. He works on your sins. He gets in your head, twisting things, turning them around on us. Most of us would rather be clothed in a lie than to be naked in the truth.

Once you start listening to his lies, the truth gets farther and farther away until you can't tell what is the truth and what is a lie. That is when you start taking the easy way out, or what fits you.

Hopefully, one day, we find faith in God. We give him our life completely. Then with God, Jesus, and the Holy Spirit, we can go back and reclaim what we gave the enemy. I am so new at this life. I'm trying to understand God's way. I'm learning all the time. Everyday, he shows me something new.

This life is so amazing. I wish this life for all. I have prayed to God, asked him why he doesn't do for others what he did for me. I keep getting the same answer thy will.

One night, he explained to me. He said that I had given up on life. I was disgusted with the person that I was. I had no will left to live that I so freely handed my whole life to him. I handed him everything not trying to hold back a single thing. He knew just what I would do with the miracle he gave me, the beautiful gift of new life.

He took me from the darkness so fast. He ripped me out of my old self, my old ways. All of the bad was gone, left in the pit with the old me. He sat my feet on solid ground, picked up my head so I could see, and blessed me with a blessing that would last a lifetime.

To live is Christ and to fail is death. I choose Christ. He gave his life for me. The mercy and love he has to be able to give his life for someone, someone that doesn't believe in him. This is the kind of love Jesus has for all.

His love is my other gift. It changed me, flooded my heart until I had to share with others. This love, God's love, is so amazing. What we as humans believe to be love, we're not even close. His love is everything. It's everywhere. It never ends and it never fails. No matter what we do or have done, he still loves us.

Even in the worst part of my life, he was right there by my side. He was waiting for me. All I had to do was call out to him. He had so much grace and love for someone that totally denounce him. Even after all of the stuff I had done he still chose me. He poured his love in me and gave me a new life. This is the awesome part. It's so undeniable and indescribable at the same time. I try and try to describe it and all I get is that we have no idea what love is until we give our lives to God. He shows us true love.

My life today is God's life. I live to serve. Anything God wants, I'm here for him. There are no questions anymore like why me, I'm not worthy, I'm still broken, or you're still fixing me. When he chose me, he had a reason. It's some great plain for me. Yes, I have a reason to live now. I am one of his chosen. I truly believe this with all of my heart.

Everything in me is of God. I know that I can't ever say no to him for any reason. God's love is in my heart to stay. The Holy spirit runs through my body in my blood. The power of Jesus is in me. I know this is true. I feel it everyday.

Think about this. The most important part of a jig-saw puzzle is the missing piece, the one you have to look for. You leave all of the others to find that one. At that time, it is more important than all of the others. How happy are you when you find it? Now think about how Jesus says to leave the 99 to find that one. Think about how God felt when you opened up to him.

How did you feel when you found your way to him? Think about this. Did you feel like the most important part was finally put in place? Life was made so beautiful, right? Did you come to know his love? Was your heart flooded with his love? Did his Grace, Mercy, and Love overwhelm you? Does your happiness keep growing every day? Can you feel his love in your heart? Have you been changed? Are you now living a new life? It's so amazingly beautiful, right? Now don't you wish that everyone would do this. I wish that everyone I come in contact with would come to know God's love. I wish that they would let God redeem them because this life is what dreams are made of. I could never have dreamed that I would be writing this or even living this life.

I really believed that I was going to be an addict until I died. It's a good thing that God had other plans for me. I see so much that he is doing to me.

Now I understand why he does what he does. It's so that he can get things done here on Earth. Things that have to be done. You see this is why he uses us to work through. When we are on Earth we can't see his face. We get that privilege when we go home. Until then, we are a door for his love to enter the earth.

I know his love is in me. I feel the Holy Spirit running around inside me. I can feel his love pour out of me. I can see it touch others. I get the privilege to see a smile enter a face. Has this ever happened to you? Do you ever have a bad day then see someone that makes you smile? That feeling at that moment is God touching you.

Now imagine that feeling all day, every day. What a beautiful way to live. Just knowing God is right by your side. Then he starts talking to you. Some can even feel him touch them. Isn't this awesome to know God's love and to truly believe he is always with you? No matter what you do, his love will never stop.

Please stop running away from him. Just take a chance with God. When you do, you will wish you had done it a long time ago. I know because I do. Let God's love in. You will definitely be changed. Start enjoying a new way of life.

It's here for the asking. God wants to give you this gift. Do you really want it? If you do just say the words. I need you lord. I give you my life. I'm all yours. Now in the time I have come to know Christ, I realize that even when I didn't believe, he was right there for me.

So many things that happen in my life shows me that it had to be God. I can think back to when I was 4. I went into Mom and Dad's bedroom. I got one of Mom's bobby pins and stuck it in the electric plug. I should have been dead. It threw me back so hard into the bed that it knocked the life back into me.

I remember when I was five and running through a field. I fell and cut my thumb off. The doctors said that I wouldn't use my hand again. Well, God was there.

God healed me even when he knew I was going to be an addict. He knew that I would denounce him over and over and that I would go through life not believing in him. How about all of the times that I OD'd? Yes, God was there. Even when I tried to kill myself, he was there.

God, It's amazing how you can take a broken down, has been, nothing and change me into one of your chosen. When you hear God fixes broken things, believe me he does. I was so broken. I was lost with no way back. I was already dead. Now, God gives me strength to handle all situations. His love pours from me onto others. His forgiveness is always working through me, and in me. God truly holds my life in his hands.

Let me explain some things. That happened in my life. You see, I have learned that God has always been with me. No matter how much I didn't believe, he was still working through me.

Many years ago, before my son was born, I was driving down the street. I saw a pickup truck flip over and start burning in my rear view mirror. I stopped, got out, and ran over to it. I jumped up on it and tried to open the door, but it was locked. I broke the window out, opened the door, and reached in to pull the man out. He was drunk and started fighting me. Somehow, I managed to get him out. When we hit the ground, I looked up and saw the fire coming out of the door. At that time, I didn't know why I did this. I really didn't care about others. Now I know that it was God working in me.

When I think back, there was no fear in me. All that mattered was getting that man out of that truck. See, this was God. Now try to imagine this one.

My son and I were out doing some bait fishing and walking along the Creek. He was five then. He really loved to go fishing with me. You have to remember my son couldn't see real good. I didn't like to have him around the lakes or rivers. We had a great day.

Walking back to the car, I still can't remember all that happened. We were 10 foot above the creek. The ground gave way under his feet. The amazing thing is that I had a hold of his hand before he was past ground level. Everything in my hands were gone. I still don't know how I knew he was falling. Yes I do. It was God.

You see, God has always been working in me even when I didn't believe in him. As much hurt that I caused him while telling people there is no God, he never left me. He's always been there helping me or working through me.

It was my eyes that couldn't see, my heart that wouldn't open up to him. I was so lost living with the devil and believing I had a good life. I would tell everyone that I was happy. Yeah right, drinking and drugging. That is what I called a happy life.

I fell a few times, but I always built myself back up. I had a house, cars, and even a truck. I had all of this while using. I had good jobs and worked hard, but I was living the lies of the world. I believed everyone of them too.

The devil had me right where he wanted me. He was giving me what I wanted so that he could keep me in his grip. That's what he does. He lets us have things we want so that he can hold on to us. I know that I would follow that drug anywhere it wanted to take me. It really didn't matter what I had to do. Lying, Cheating, stealing, and robbing among other things. I told you that I was a bad person.

I can remember being at a person's house. We were really messed up big time after hours of partying. Then this girl OD'd. Everyone starts leaving, this girl is turning blue. I go over to her and start doing CPR. Never in my life have I had a lesson on how to do it, but I knew what to do. I did CPR until the life squad got there. They said I saved her life.

I saw her a week later at a party. She did say thanks for saving her life as she put a needle in her arm. See the life I lived? We didn't care about anyone or anything. Not even ourselves. Just so you know, that girl died a month later. When I was told, I just said I believe it. That was cold of me.

I really didn't understand any of this, but now I do. It's God's amazing hand at work. We just don't see it until we are walking with him. Then we can see how he is everywhere, in everything. It's not that we had to find God. He wasn't gone or lost. We had to find our way to God. We are the ones that were lost. We walked away from him. Some of us even ran.

When we can stop running and open the door, God's love will fill our hearts beyond what it can handle. We have to let it flow out of us. Yes, God put a million billion doors on this Earth for his love to flow through. You are one of those doors.

I'm going to tell you some things that most people don't know about me. You see, I was so far gone in that life. Nothing mattered to me except getting high. What we called getting well then.

The one thing that really gets me is when my Mom died. I didn't really feel anything. I always wondered why. Now I know. Nothing in me worked. I was on cruise control. Just existing not living. I really don't think I even cried when she passed. Now if I think about her, the tears don't stop. So am I a bad person for not grieving then? I used to think I was. Until my sister said something to me one day.

My sister believes Mom had a talk with God about me. Yes, God already knew everything. It's the love that is shown that he listens to. My sister said that they had a very long talk about who I was and who I was meant to be. God made me for a reason. I have a purpose. God is using me for something very big. He has been preparing me all these years.

Look at me now. I'm somebody my mom would be proud to call her son. A man that did a complete change and don't look back. My life is with God now. I went from trying to kill myself to trying to live God's way. I'm so full of happiness and love. Thank you Lord for your gift of life and listening to the love from my mother.

Mom, God has you now. Hold on to your love I'm coming to see you. I love you!!!

God is amazing. I got his life in exchange for mine. That was the gift he gave me. Sitting on that bunk that night. Did I deserve it? No. Did I expect it? No. I had no idea what I was in for. I woke up a different person.

God gave me new life. He actually redeemed me. I really believe that if I was to go back to that life, first, I would be throwing everything back in God's face. I'd be saying that it's not worth anything. Second, I would be dead now. This is why I had to give up everything, all of the people I called friends, and my marriage too. It was all about using.

If I went back to that life, I would be in the grave now. God is the saver of my life. The things he does for me and through me is so awesome to see. His hand at work in my life as well as others. When God wants you he will never let go. I know I have put him through a lot. He has fought the enemy a long time for me. Now the war is over. God wins.

God's grace and love is so amazing. Just knowing that he took a worthless nothing and turned me into a child of God with a purpose for living. Yes, we hear this all the time. When you get it and live it, it's so awesome. Especially after all the years of living in the darkness.

That is where I lost all sense of hope. I didn't live anymore I just existed. That is what drugs and living the wrong way will do to you. When you listen to the lies the enemy tells you, the most important things in your life become pointless.

God saved me from the grave. I was already dead. There is no other way I would be telling you this except for the grace of God. The life I used to think was right was so far off. It's because we as people take things and hide them in our head. We put them in a grave inside our minds until we forget about them.

That doesn't stop the scars those things have already made in our lives or the pain we live with over something we try to hide from everyone and most importantly ourselves. Our minds are very complex. The things I put in the grave in my mind were gone from memory until I started working the step study books in celebrate recovery. God said he had some things for me to do. The amazing thing is I follow his way and life is so beautiful.

Celebrate Recovery is a program that anyone and everyone should be doing. With God's help, I have dug up things I put to rest a long time ago. The things that I didn't remember. God was there saying you forgot this over here. That was the one that hurt the most. When I uncovered it, all those memoirs were right in my face. It was so overwhelming.

I felt God's hand on my shoulder and he said he loves me. We all know that good and bad things will happen to understand that God has all things no matter what. Then you start to see God's will. Believe me, he only wants good for us. Some things do hurt and he knows, but those are the ones that have to be done. Sometimes for others, sometimes for us.

Trust God. He is our strength, our guide, our power, our life, and our love. I'm still learning God's love. Its got to be the most incredible thing I have ever tried to learn. The joy, the happiness that's in his love is so overwhelming. You can lose yourself in his love. It must be why they say it's the kind of love God only knows. It's definitely the most beautiful thing to ever touch my heart.

God tells me to love others as he loves. That's a lot of love. To really be able to do this, we have to know God's love. When we feel it pour out of us, the joy and the happiness. The Holy Spirit runs wild in us. That's God's love. It is forever.

God has done some amazing things in my life like putting Brittany in my life. She showed me kindness, caring, and love. She opened her heart to me and showed me that a woman can love me without wanting something. She is a beautiful young woman that means the world to me.

The love I have for Brittany, I never felt this kind of love. I would give my life for her without hesitation. She is the daughter I never had. To think that her heart opened my eyes to the way I think about women.

God does things that can't be explained. He puts people in our lives for reasons unknown to us. God tells me to enjoy all he does and to not ask questions about what he does or why.

Everything happens for a reason. I will do all I can to live as he wants me to. I want Christ in me more and more until all of me is gone. I want the fire in me to shine so bright that the whole world can see. My life is his, so I know if it's meant to be then it will be.

God's love, Grace, and his will are more powerful than anything of this earth. God put me on this path. I'm walking and talking his way the best I can. I know everything that I want is this way. I love all that God does for me. I love my new life. I will fight for this life just like God fought for me.

Jesus died on the cross for me. He took my sins and washed me clean. He redeemed me. His love is undeniable and indescribable at the same time. It's so awesome feeling it working in me every day. Now I have been asked if I would give up my life to save someone else. My answer is yes. I would in a heartbeat. As much as I love it, I would give it away to save another life. I know this is true because it comes from my heart.

My heart is full of God's love. This is a different feeling for me. I know that I'm blessed beyond all measures by God. I now know that the impossible becomes possible. With God, all things are possible. God tells me to love others as he loves me. This is what I do every day because without love I'm nothing.

I wish I could break off pieces of my life to give to others because if they could experience it for a moment, feel God's love pour into them, it would change them.

People, if we ever want to see the face of God, we are going to have to believe 100% that Jesus Christ died on the cross for us and that all things are possible in God's hands.

Jesus, thank you for the salvation. The freedom is something I've never known. The gift of a new life is so amazing. The people you put in my life mean so much to me. God, you know everything. One day I would love to sit and talk about all you do. You are what I seek all day every day. Please let your love flow out on the ones that need it like you did me. Flood their hearts.

God, I want to thank you for the new life you have blessed me with. Thank you for your Grace and Mercy you shower us with. Thank you for all the love you poured into me. Thank you for the Holy Spirit that lives inside us. I know with everything in me that you have truly redeemed me. Thank you Lord Jesus. Amen.

Finding You

People are asking why God doesn't talk to them. Well people, you know that voice in your head? The one saying you know that is wrong. You shouldn't do that. That's the Holy Spirit. He speaks the words of God. That is the one you should listen to.

The other one is the enemy. He lies to you. He tells you that it's ok. Nobody will know but you. You're just doing it to yourself. You're not hurting anybody. We believe the lies taught to us growing up such as take the easy way out. You know what it's actually harder to live that old life then it is to live this new life.

God does talk to all of us. We have to be wise enough to understand him. Wise enough to be able to distinguish which voice is his. Wise enough to know that his voice is truth and what is right!

Some of us try too hard to hear his voice. We end up blocking it out. Others just don't listen. They really don't care. They just want to do their thing. Look, if it's of God, it's truth and right. You know this already, but still choose to do your thing even when you know his words can set you free. You even pray to Him asking for Him to help you. Then, when the help is in front of you, you make up excuses, turn your back, say your not ready. Anything you can to get away.

Just stop and think. If this is really the life you want, is it not worth everything in this world to you? If you want it that much, would you not give up everything? Can you walk away from that life knowing that you have a brand-new beautiful life ahead of you.

A life filled with happiness, joy, freedom, forgiveness, and love. Can you see yourself living a life like that? A life where you don't worry about things. You're not stressed out everyday. You don't have to worry about where you are going to get your next fix at or how.

Once you turn your life over to God, the holy spirit that he gives us will guide us along or path. Yes, the holy spirit is how God communicates with us. If you say you don't hear God talking to you, you're wrong. You're just not listening to him.

For real people, I'm here to guide you. God said I am to save people. Yes, I'm here for you and you. I'm just a vessel God works through, one of his many doors to let his love into this cruel world. You really need to see with your heart. Listen and hear what your heart and eyes are telling you. God is the only one. Stop saying you're not ready when for real you could never be more ready than you were the first time you thought about Jesus.

Let's do a quick check.

Do you have hope in God? Do you have faith in God?

Do you believe that Jesus died on the cross for you?

To take your sins away to wash you clean with his blood? Do you know he has forgiven you?

So now why do you think you're not ready? You're listening to the wrong voice again.

Let God and the Holy Spirit take over and guide you. Start listening to the holy spirit. He speaks the words of God. He will never steer you wrong or put you in danger. Yes, God forgives us. Yes, God feels your pain. Some even brings tears to his eyes. The thing that hurts the most is knowing that he can't stop some from what they do.

You see, first you have to understand. We all have this thing called free will. That means that we can do what we want even if it hurts others. Do you believe that God doesn't feel your pain? That he just sits there not caring about you. The thing is, God knows what will happen before it does.

He also knows he can't stop it from happening, to stop us from hurting others. He would have to take away our free will. Then what do we become? A puppet that can't choose what we do. Without free will, we can only do what we're told to do. Is this how you believe life should be? How you believe God should treat us? Make us into a puppet that he controls. You really don't think God wants every one of us with him? He knows we have to make the choice to come to him.

When I wrote this, I really wasn't thinking about how saying these things about people could hurt. My heart was feeling bad about the words I used, so I had to add these few lines. I really don't know what else to call them. How to describe the way these people are.

This world is full of backstabbing two-faced people. It's so funny when they sit and talk about each other. When one is not around, the other can't stop acting like they are the biggest piece of garbage. Yes, talking bad about the other. Then when they are together, they're best friends.

Why do they have to do this? Does the truth hurt that much, or is it that they are just that fake that they don't want the other to know how they feel about them. I can honestly say that I have found it so much easier to just tell the truth.

With God in me, I can't lie anymore. This is why I see things differently. It's because when all of the lies come out, people get hurt, so why lie in the first place. I tell people how I feel. If they choose to not say anything to me, that is on them. Does it hurt? Yes. Will I lose sleep over it? No because if they just talk about it to me, then they will find forgiveness.

I don't hold anything over anyone. I'm one of the first to forgive, so if someone has something against me, it's on them. Look, we humans don't care about hurting others or even ourselves. For real, humans don't think about our actions and what they do to others. Most of the time we don't even care what we do. We don't care how it makes others feel because humans are selfish only care about ourselves.

We really know nothing about love. When we give our lives to God is when we start to care about others. That is when we see the pain we have caused others. We really start to understand God's way.

Is it right for us to blame God for the actions of other humans? I tell you no, it's not. I tell you the pain you went through, God was there. He was crying with you.

How can you truly say that God lets things happen when he can't stop somebody from doing something. If it's what they want to do, they're going to do it because of free will. I understand there's a lot of pain here. We just have to get up, come to God. Please just understand that God feels your pain too. Don't ever give up. Stay with him. He will always be there by your side. Yes he loves you forever no matter what.

His son, Jesus Christ made this way for us. Now you really have to look at it this way. God knows all about pain. He gave his son to the world knowing that he would be tortured, and hung on a cross to die. How would you be able to hand over your kid knowing this. Then look at the pain that Jesus had to go through. Beaten and tortured and hung on a cross. All for the sins of this world, our sins, mine and yours.

He did it out of love for us, you and me. His words were father forgive them for they know not what they do. Is this not total forgiveness, true love for all mankind. Now we blame Him for the things that another human does to us or to their self. Stop shaking your fist at God. It all falls back on free will. Just believe that with God, happiness is there. Without God, we are doomed to. I can tell you this.

The Bible says that when Jesus comes back, it will be like a thief in the night. Do you truly understand that? A thief in the night comes unnoticed. You really don't know until it's to late. It's already over before you know it. To me that means if your not with God, then you won't be going to heaven because you definitely won't have time to change.

Remember, it's over before you know about it. For real people, make your move now. God is on the move, so hop on board with him now. Don't wait until it's too late. Come be a child of God. Accept his gift of life.

Now when you get down to it, our problems are not as big as we thought. For real, we are bigger than they are, so why do we let things get us down. Should we not be trying our best to find good in everything? I truly believe that everything happens for a reason. God's plans are not known to us until we walk through it and understand his will. That is when we know why.

It's truly amazing how God can use us for certain things even if we don't agree with it at the time. We don't understand, but God knows the outcome. This is a true act of love. When we can just do what he gives us. No hesitation no thinking about it. Really, don't try to talk yourself out of doing what God wants. If God is telling you to do something, you can bet your life that it's a good thing. It is to help you or others. Maybe both you and others.

Sometimes we have to do what has to be done for the better of others. God only gives you what he knows you can handle. We may not see it that way at that time. We might struggle with it or even be hurt. Once we get through it and look back, we see why he chose us and then we realize it had to be me. This burden could destroy a lot more than it has.

Thank you, God, for giving me the strength to do your will. Sometimes we have to do what we believe is wrong to help someone else. Ok, first, maybe that is the only way they can see and learn. Then is it what God wants or what you want? Will God say it had to be done or will he have to clean up the mess you made? There is this one too. Is it the devil telling you to do it acting like God? Choose wisely my friend.

I'm going to be honest with you. I really do want to go to heaven, but truthfully, I would spend the rest of eternity in the devils playground just to know that I helped someone get to heaven. That would make it alright to me because there's nothing that's going to steal my joy. ("Not even the devil")

It is truly amazing how we sometimes beat ourselves up over something we did, when we should find the good in that situation. We start making the best out of every opportunity. Our lives will get better. I know this now. No matter how many chains they throw on me, or how far down they pull me, I'm coming back stronger than ever because God gave me a new life, and I have the blood of Jesus in me. Now nothing can stop me.

How many of us think to ourselves, why did God do this to me? I'm here to tell you that what God did for me is nothing short of a miracle. Yes, I have been blessed beyond all measures. Yes, I know this and believe this with everything in my head, heart and soul. Now let me get back to the question.

You just don't know. We can't help wondering if we are special. Are we truly that different from everybody else or is it just that we recognize our purpose in life? Yes, the one that God gave to us.

See, I asked why me because I knew there were others more worthy, ones that deserved to have this life more than me. With all of the bad I did in my life, I don't know how anybody could love me this much, but yes, God says he does love me. He says I am worthy of all he does. He says I am special to him, and that I am priceless. I have a purpose, something that I have to do for God. Now that is the reason right there.

God has something I have to do for him. My life today is to help people. Sometimes the people we help really need it, then there's others that just want to try and use your kindness as a weakness.

I was told this once by a wise man. If I offer, then I'm not being used. I have had to understand that the things I do for others is not always a good thing to do. In other words, I had to learn to say no. There are times when I know that some are going to do the wrong thing. I keep trying to tell them that I have lived that life and I have done everything they are doing. I know the lies told to get what is wanted. They can think that they are getting over on me, but I know.

You see, sometimes the best thing we can do for others is to not do anything at all. Yes, it took me some time to understand this. It took until the day God said to me unanswered prayers. Then I saw what he was saying. The things people want are not always what they need. I was trying to please people instead of helping which can open the door to a lot of being taken advantage of.

Ok yes, I did have other reasons with some. I understand now that they were just going through the motions. Yes, it makes me look at them different now, but then when I think about it, I'm not any better. I was there for that reason too, so now I have to ask for forgiveness. Not only for them, but for me too. Did I think about it at the time, no. I really didn't understand what was happening. I was just going through the motions too.

When you give your heart so easily, people tend to walk on it. Some even stomp on it. It doesn't make sense to me when someone says they love you then turn around and crush your heart. Yes, God has told me to guard my heart. I'm doing the best I can, but there are some that we care about so much that it doesn't matter what they do. We will always be there for them even if they crush our heart.

I know that love is a beautiful thing, but yes, sometimes it can hurt more than anything. God tells me to be strong. To live life like Jesus. Love all people, everyone. Believe me it took me time to understand this. It took until I realized I don't have to like them to love them.

You see, even the ones we love are going to do things we don't agree with and things we don't like. Everyone is different in what they do or what they say. This used to bother me. I just had to realize that I'm not here to please anybody. I really don't care what people think of me now. The only one that I care about what they think of me is God. He gives me the best advice. He is always there to help me. He is the one I get my love from. Now I know that love means that sometimes we have to say no. That we can't do everything that is asked for. Sometimes the best thing is nothing.

I know that God is always there for me even in the hardest parts of life. If I just stop and look, I will find him there. He is waiting for me with his hands out. He will pick me up or guide me, whatever is needed at the time. We just have to open our eyes to see. I have thought that my eyes were wide open. The most amazing thing is that my eyes still open more each day.

Today, the things I do hopefully reflect my life with God. Everything I am is of God. All I want is to be full of the Holy Spirit, to be the one that walks down the street and people see Jesus.

I want to spread his love all over this earth. I really do want all to know how beautiful this life is. You see, God is amazing in all he does. Yes, he created us in his image. He gave us life on this earth, so why do we forget this? Some of us don't care and some don't believe. I know I never believed.

Does this hurt God? I think it does. It would hurt anyone to watch their children go the wrong way, so why do we do this? We do this because we think the wrong way is the fun way. You know, I can talk about this for a long time. I lived the wrong way for a lot of years. So let's not get into this.

Now lets see, strike one is not believing. Strike two is living the wrong way. Now the big one, strike three is telling people that there is no God. By all rights, he should have left me in stuck in Satan's world. After all, I was already dead. My life was over, well what I thought was life. I tried so many times to end it, but you know what? God had other plans for me.

The day I had a glimmer of hope, just the littlest piece of faith, I asked for help from God because I had tried everything else by then. God was very quick at pulling me out of Satan's domain. Yes, me, someone that didn't believe in him. He gave me the miracle of a new life with all of his amazing gifts that overwhelmed me. Forgiveness, happiness, joy, and his love. He flooded my heart with his love, showed me what true love is. It is something I thought I knew. I was so far off.

Let me tell you this. God gives us so many gifts. We are the ones that need to recognize them. All the gifts he has given me. It really did take time to understand them, to know they happened because of God. Look I have a beautiful awesome life now.

Yes, I owe it all to God.

His gifts to me have come in the form of many things, but the most important thing was the angels he sent to help me. I know when I'm being helped. All I can do is thank God for all he does. Now that I am stronger in my walk with him, I can look back at my old life and see where he was there for me. Amazing how the God of all was always there by my side even when I didn't believe in him.

Can you believe he stayed by my side when I would tell people there is no God? Yes, now I know why. It's because he is God and he loves everyone. It doesn't matter what you have done or what you are doing. God will never leave you. So when you are broken down and beat up, tired of life, and just want to give up, try asking God for help.

I'm here to tell you this- look at me. He saved me from a life with the devill. I was really stuck there with no way out. The really bad thing is that I didn't care. All I wanted to do was die. Please just look at this. If God can do this for me, what do you think he can do for you?

Sometimes, God does things for us that we don't understand. His amazing gifts come in so many ways. It is up to us to be able to see and understand these gifts. Sometimes it can be an opportunity. Sometimes a person is sent to help us. Sometimes it's just a little thing.

Sometimes it can be an angel.

Then there is always his gifts of love, grace, mercy, happiness, and joy. It is so easy for me to see what he does. I sometimes don't think about how hard it is for others. When God opens your eyes to his ways, you will see more of what he does. You will understand more, then you start to see his hand at work in your life as well as others.

Your gift has been with you for some time now. It will not go away, but you have to be able to find it, understand why and knowing why will come. Don't try to push it. God has done some things through me that are unexplainable. Now he is still doing things, but he is telling me before he does. Still, there are times when he sends me without saying a thing to me, but more often now, he is telling me.

The feeling I get when I help someone find their way. I'm thinking how to describe it. I can't find the right words. This is definitely from God. How many of us can describe anything God does? 'None' I can tell you this much for sure. God only wants good for us, so now it is your time.

Just think about where you need God in your life. Are you willing to put your life in God's hands? Are you willing to give him complete control? Can you live a life where God is your first priority?

Can you really let him handle all your ups and downs? Live a stress free life with no worries, no shame, and no regrets.

You see, I truly do this. My life is full of love, happiness, and joy. I have been told that I can't really let him have everything. For real people, I do. God takes care of all for me. My ups and downs, my pain, and sorrow. Yes, he even takes care of the things that pop up every day. Believe me, it's not that it just happens. I had to truly understand what God does and why before I could really get to this place in my walk with him. I'm really surprised that it has happened so fast for me. I know that I have complete trust in the lord. I know that whatever he does is for the best.

When something hurts me. I look for what I need to learn from it. I know that everything he does is to better us and teach us. Most importantly I know his love for me. And I love him above all. After all he did take a dead man and give me life. A real reason to live.

I know that I am wanted and loved. I know that he fought the devil for me. Even when I didn't believe in him, he was there with me. Let me tell you why I like to see smiles on people. It's something about joy and happiness.

Yes this is true- but I know the day that I gave my life to God, he had a smile on his face. I have not been able to see that yet, but I will. I really do want to put a smile on everyone's face. Just knowing the power of a little smile. Amazing how something that is free can change how we feel.

Everything I believe in is of God. Everything I do is of God. Everything I am is of God. I am here to help others find their way to God. He is putting me where I need to be all the time.

I am over all of my past. God took it away. He cleaned me. Every step I take is with God. He is everything. He is my life. My path with him is so bright. His light shines on me all of the time. Yes, sometimes I stumble and sometimes I fall, but he is right there picking me up and brushing me off. Putting my feet back on the path. And telling me he still loves me.

This is the God that wants you too. He wants everyone to know him and his ways, to come back to what you were made for, to be a child of God, and to know you are loved. He is with you and will never leave you.

Do you know how amazing it is to know that you are walking this earth as a child of God? Just knowing that he has great plans for you. So many awesome things he will have you do. Just knowing your walking this earth as others have, and doing as God wants.

It's so amazing to really understand this. Most people don't have a clue that God has chosen us. What I'm trying to say is that we are different. Some people can see it in you. You can feel it. You know it, but that doesn't compare to knowing God has chosen you, that he has something very special for you to do.

This is what I feel and know every day. I know that God has great plans for me, that I am to do something very special for him. This is the reason I'm having a hard time with not wanting to let him down. He keeps telling me that I have been preparing for this my whole life, that everything I went through was for this reason. God says to remember all even what he has shown me.

I will need all of my wisdom and knowledge. The devil will try everything to stop me. Even stuff I have not seen before. When I hear this it brings fear of letting him down. I don't want to fail. Then I hear, you can't. I chose you - you are a victor. Do you know how that feels to have God tell you this? Nothing could ever be better.

The best part of all of this is that he knows everything. He knows what will happen before it happens. So why do I fear failure? That is the human in me. Sorry, but as a human, I was always a failure. God has changed me now. I'm his child. When he says I will not fail, the only thought should be that God knows everything.

See we all have a purpose in life, a reason for being here. Some of us have something to do that's going to impact the future. Others don't even care about what God made them for.

I know that I used to be one of them until that day God pulled me out of the darknessl and showed me that I had a reason. He changed my life so fast I really didn't know what happened. I found myself asking why me why would you do this to me. Then came that day he made everything clear to me. You can believe this much.

When God does something, it's not for us to question. He knows exactly what he's doing. Yes, he has known from the beginning. A very long time before you were born he knew. It's just that free will of ours. It gets in our way. It's unpredictable. We make a choice and it throws our future out of whack. Even to this day, there are two roads for every life. It is your choice as to which road you go down.

Keep your choices going God's way. Listen to the Holy Spirit. Follow him in the way of Jesus and we will not fail. No more asking why me. Just do what God made you to do. That other road, I lived on it all of my B.C. life. It's not a good place to spend a lifetime. We all know where that road leads. It leads to a life of destruction, shame and guilt.

With God, life changes. You get happiness, joy, and love. Will it be hard? Sometimes, yes, but it is so worth it. God has told me to stop asking why and enjoy what he gives me. If you really stop and think about it, this is a story of Resurrection because the old me died and the new me was born.

I used to believe that you couldn't get clean if you trade one addiction for another, but I'm here to tell you that I traded all my addictions for one. I'm addicted to God's love. It's truly the most incredible thing to ever come into my heart. I could never have known true freedom if I didn't go through that life of captivity.

Yes, I had to go through that life, all the pain, sorrow, hurt, guilt, and shame just to know what real redemption feels like. I had to really feel God's forgiveness before I could ever forgive. Truly knowing all of God's love that's in me and having lived that past life. That is what keeps me on the right path.

Why would I ever want to go back to Satan's world? God pulled me out of there and I gave him my life. In exchange he gave me his life. Yes I truly know what redemption, freedom, and forgiveness feels like now. I'm here to tell you it's a beautiful life full of happiness, joy, and love.

The Holy Spirit is definitely working over time in me. Everything in me, about me, and what I do is of God. I talk to him for his guidance, knowledge, and wisdom. He always lets me know if I'm doing right or wrong. You see, to God, I am priceless.

God is the one that has shown me my worth. God gave me this life so that I can go out and help others. He made me see that to be worth anything, you have to first be worth everything to yourself. Forgive yourself of all your past. God already has. When you really do this, then you will overcome shame and guilt. You start to feel yourself becoming new. You start to understand the love God has for you, see how he values your life, and how you truly are the one he has left the 99 for.

You see, God has never stopped. We are the ones that went out and forgot him. We left without saying anything to him. We just turned our backs and walked away. Here is where we find our worth. After all we done to God, he is right there with arms spread wide open, and love pouring all over us.

You are worth so much to God. He sacrificed his only son for us. Jesus gave his life for us. Do you see your worth here? Please never let someone tell you that you are worthless. God says you are priceless. That means that you are worth more than anything. Nothing of this world is worth more than you. Now you just found out your worth, but is this where it stops or do you continue to grow with God.

When you grow, your worth grows. Are you truly going to walk under his guidance? Allow God to control your life. Give everything you are to him not holding back anything. He already knows everything anyway. Now embrace your new life and your new found worth. You have a purpose in life. It's time to do what God has planned for you.

Let's take a look at this world through God's eyes, how much pain we cause him. His love for us is beyond our comprehension. Our human brain can't even imagine the kind of love he has for us. How much love would have to be in you to send your child to be tortured and hung on a cross for us humans to have forgiveness of our sins, and to have a way to God, to be washed by the blood of Jesus Christ, and accept the Holy Spirit as our guide in life.

See, God give us all of this as a gift of life. I have seen so many people take advantage of God's gifts. Yes there are the ones that don't understand. They're the ones that when it happens to them, they get scared because of the newness. For real, God wants all to come to him. So when he's looking down on us watching us, seeing the things that we do, you think this doesn't hurt him.

When we disrespect him, throw all the gifts back in his face, that's like telling him we'd rather live with Satan than to be with him. I have thought about this a long time. If we make the commitment to be saved, then why would we go out and sin again.

Jesus says come to me and sin no more. This is true salvation. When you are with God, following his way, listening to the Holy Spirit, you will not sin. It is written in Matthew. He who asks will receive. He who searches will find. He who knocks the door will be opened, and then for God's children that are down and out, there is love. "He who haves shall give". This is God's way.

My God has given me some amazing gifts. My writings is one of his gifts. His words flow from me for others to read. His love has poured into me, changed me. My love for others so indescribable. Why do we humans have to mess this world up? It is God's garden of Eden, so why do we let the devil rule here?

We gave this world to Satan. We listen to his lies. We believe his ways are the way to live until we honestly have a relationship with Jesus Christ, and we accept him as our Lord and savior. That is when all the lies become clear to us, when we understand the ways of the world. What we call man's way, and it's really Satan's way.

How much longer are we going to let this happen? Living the way of the world in Satan's hands. I believe it's time for us to open our eyes and see. It's time to live God's way. I'm here to tell you people that we're running out of time. God is on the move for a reason. Open your hearts to him. Let him show you what is really going on around you. God only wants good for you. Are you truly afraid of good and the truth?

I'm telling you there's going to be no in between. It's either God's way or the devils way. Will you give him complete control, not holding on to anything? Jump completely in. It's all of God or none of God. It really is a 100% commitment or none at all.

If you can't say that you believe, then go do your thing. Just remember what is said in Revelation 3:15-16. God says that he would rather you be hot or cold, but since you are lukewarm, he will spit you out. Do you understand this? Get off the fence. For real, we don't have much time left. God said time is running out. Stop playing with his blessings. You know his ways and still do your thing. Why? People want to hear more about the wrongs you have done than what you are doing right. They don't want to hear about how God fixes things. They'd rather hear about how the devil controls and destroys. They're stuck in the ways of the world. See things through the eyes of the world.

Yes, I've had guns held to my head and knives put to my throat. Yes, I have done so much worse to others. You see, I'm no better than anyone. I have been in the penitentiary's, jails, and yes, a lot of rehabs. Nothing ever worked for me. Did I quit using? Yes I did, but just for a little while. For real, I never got it out of my head, always thinking about it and ways to beat the system. Why? It's because I was an addict. I really thought I was happy with who I was.

Are these the things you want to hear about? How drugs and lies that the world tells us warps our minds and we lose sight of right and wrong? If you came to hear about my past, sorry I'm here to tell you about God and all of his amazing gifts. All of my past has been washed clean, so if you want to hear about it, go back to the past. I don't live there anymore.

You know, I heard this once. If Satan keeps trying to get you to look at your past, you can bet there must be something very special he doesn't want you to see in the future because he knows if you look in your past long enough, he has a chance to get a hold of you.

You see, all he needs is a little thread. He'll keep pulling and pulling until he gets you close enough. Then before you know it, you're sucked into the pit of darkness. Yes, God changed all of this in me. I don't look at my past anymore. I have been forgiven of my past, all of my sins. I have been washed by the blood of Jesus Christ. The old me is dead I have a new life. I have been redeemed.

Now do you see the amazing things God can do? He gives us a new life. You don't have to live that way anymore. God's love is so awesome. It is the place that we all need to live. I have had an amazing life these past few years. The things God is doing in my life are totally indescribable. How many of us can honestly say that God has changed us completely? Not one inch short of amazingly awesome redemption.

Let me tell you something my sister said to me. You see, she knows my old life. She knows the person I was and the person I am today. I had a really hard time with until I looked at it through her eyes and understood what she was saying. She said that I was a superhero because I stood up to the devil and reclaimed my freedom. Yes sis, I did, but only with the Holy Spirit,the power of Jesus Christ in me, and God standing by my side.

See, it took more than just a superhero. It took God. If not for the change of life, I would never had the strength to do it. To really look at my life now, compared to who I was, it's two totally different people, but the same person. It seems impossible, but it's true.

Only God can do this to you. Only he can take you from a worthless piece of garbage and change you into a triumphant Victor, one with a place in the kingdom of heaven. Yes, I am a child of God. Even after all the stuff I have done, he still loves me. He knows everything I have done and he's forgiven me.

It's such an amazing feeling to know that God has chosen you, that he knows your name and calls you one of his children, and that you no longer have to walk around with your head down in shame. He lifted my head and opened my eyes to see the real truth of the world.

When you have God's love in you, everything changes. If you really want this life with Jesus, then hold on. He will show you things you would have never believed before.

Thank you, God, for everyone you have put in my life, especially Brittany. I don't know if I would have understood true unconditional love if not for her. You already knew that. That's why you used her. It's so amazing to see the outcome. You really do know everything.

Now to tell you about Brittany. She is the most beautiful and kind-hearted person I have ever known. She has truly impacted my life more than words could say. I thank God everyday for putting her in my life. She is the one that no matter what she does, I'm still going to love her.

God has used her to show me a life changing understanding of his love. Why? It's because she is the daughter I never had. This is God's love inside me. This is true unconditional love!

Yes, he is telling me that I have to love all just like he loves me. This sounds so hard, but for real, my love even surprises me. I know that I can't just put my heart out freely to everyone, but I can pour love out.

God is still telling me to guard my heart. It's amazing how God works through people. This is the second time he has used Brittany to show me something. This time it was the part of his love that I didn't catch, to truly know and have unconditional love. Yes for all, everything, everybody, even the animals, and all of nature.

God made this world his garden of Eden. We were made to love and enjoy his creation, but somewhere along the line, man has tried to fade God out saying that it was created by evolution.

I know one thing. If you really stop and look at this world, you will see no way it was created by the big bang. There is just too much stuff that would take a lot of thinking such as water. Two gases combined to make a liquid, and then the soil, then the trees.

Trees breathe in carbon monoxide and put off oxygen. The very thing we need to survive. Now tell me how could this be possible. Only God's great planning could come up with the earth. Everything is in tune with the next, all working together as one. That tells you right there that it was God if you just open your eyes and understand, hear what our eyes are telling us.

Wake up people, God is everything and everywhere. He has been through more than we could ever imagine, so why do we act like our times are so hard. Could you send your son to die on a cross for the sins of others? Why take for granted all that God has done for us. We need to understand his love.

Remember that we were created in his image. This means not from apes. Evolution is the biggest lie that man has tried to teach us. My question to them is, why can't you find that missing link? You find everything else, but not what links man to apes.

Come on, stop lying to yourself. There is none. God made you live with it. Come to God, love him, give him everything you are. He will open your eyes to see, hear, and understand what he has done for you. Come find God's love. Let it in your heart. I guarantee you will be changed. Everything will be made different to you.

Yes, you can see God in everything, but then you can hear him in everything, too. When you really open your eyes, you will hear everything he has been trying to tell you all your life. Everything is God, and God is everything. I can tell you this. We have learned things all of our lives. Some right, some wrong. Please understand, God only wants good for us. He created this world for us. Is this not a good place? Every little speck of it. Created by his touch, his breath, and his word. There's so much beauty in everything. How can people say that God didn't create the earth?

They are being lied to by the enemy. Even now, everyday life is a battle. We have good lifting us up and evil trying to pull us down. The enemy will try all kinds of things just to get us to start questioning ourselves and God's words. The enemy will pull our wants and desires out. He will turn them around on us, wanting us to come to his way of thinking.

This is when we have to be strong and keep our walk with God. When we stand up to the enemy, he runs away, but only for a short time. He will never stop trying to get us. The more we walk with God, the more he tries to get a hold of us. Just some little thing, and he has you. I have come to realize that with God, the enemy has no handle on me. Just think about that for a while.

If you know there is a way to escape all your pain, all your shame, and all your guilt, what would this be worth to you? If you know there is a way out of the darkness that blocks your judgement, a way to change how you think, so you can make better choices to become free and learn forgiveness, where you have mercy and true love, what would all this be worth to you?. Would you try to get this at any cost to have a life like that? Priceless, don't you think?

Now, what if I was to tell you that it's free. Yes, it doesn't cost a thing. This life can be yours. All you have to do is ask. Wait, you do have to believe too? Just the tiniest little bit of faith. Yes, if you know of Jesus, then you know he died on the cross for our salvation. See, you already believe. It's not that hard, is it? Now that you know he died on the cross to save all of us, why are you holding back?

This is where you need to be throwing yourself at his feet. Ok, just say I need your help God, I can't do this by myself. I have no control of my life. Please help me. Take control of my life show me the way. Without you I'm nothing. I give you my life please take it in your hands. Breath in me give me new life.

I can only say this. You have to have Jesus in you not on you. You have to understand the amount of love he gives. He gives his Mercy and Grace, his happiness, his joy, and all the forgiveness and freedom. To really understand this, we have to believe with all our heart that he is the way, the truth, the life.

It's not just words that he spoke. It's so much more than that. You have to understand that he died on the cross for us. Jesus is our way to God. He is the truth and the life. His love is an amazing gift. We can never truly understand all there is to know of God's love. Our human brains can't comprehend the amount of unconditional love he so freely pours out unto us.

I keep hearing people say they're not ready. What if Jesus said I'm not ready to die on the cross. What would this world be like then? People come to the realization that we have to sacrifice. God sacrificed his son. Jesus sacrificed his life. They both did it out of love for us humans, so knowing all of this, why is it so hard for you to just say I give my life to you. Shape me, mold me, love me, I'm yours God.

Come on now, stop testing the waters and jump in the deep end. God is there! He will open your eyes. You will see he is everywhere.

He is everything. This is when you start to understand the gift that he so freely gives to us. Every day, we get his blessings.

My wish is that all could see and understand this. You know I will always be here to help others.

I am just a doorway to let his love in this sinful world.

What I understood to be love (all-wrong). What I believed to be love was only lust and self gratification. Now, I can see through new eyes. God changed so much in me. My thanking, the way I look at people, and yes, my love for everyone. God flooded my heart with his love. There is so much that I can't contain it. It just keeps pouring out.

God told me that I had to share his love with others, to love as he loves. I try and try. At first I would say that I couldn't show love until I loved someone. God told me to look at my new life, how different I am, how I will help others, and how I care about others. Then he said to me, this is love. That is when I looked up the definition of love.

— The act of caring and giving to someone else. Having someone's best interest and wellbeing as a priority in your life. To truly love is a very selfless act. Read this from 1 Corinthians 13. Love is patient, love is kind. It does not envy, it does not boast, it is not proud. 5 It does not dishonor others, it is not self-seeking, it is not easily angered, it keeps no record of wrongs. 6 Love does not delight in evil but rejoices with the truth. 7 It always protects, always trusts, always hopes, always perseveres.

Was I surprised, so I started learning all I could about his love. Wow, God's love is everything and everywhere. There is nothing in this world that is greater than his love. Yes, he blessed me with his love more than I can handle myself. This is exactly why I do what God says. I share his love. Now you have some of it because if you are reading this, then God's love is in you.

Come on now, you know me. My love is God's love. Everything I am today is because of God. His love is truly never failing. Yes, it will last forever. Just look at history. See how far back his love goes. It's still here for us, right? God's love will be around long after we are gone. I can only pray that I show his love to everyone I can reach.

Many don't want his love, some don't understand it, and others run from it. These are the ones we have to pray for. We have to keep showing them his love, keep being nice to the ones that are not nice to us. Let God's love work on their hearts.

To truly understand God's love is an amazing thing. You have to understand God's love is in everything he does, even if we don't like it or it hurts us. The truth is, it only hurts because of love. When we can understand his love, we start seeing that these things have to happen. It is God's will.

Look for the good in all things. Take your emotions out of the situation and look at it through God's eyes. We know God can do all things. Is it for God, or is it for us that we are asking of him? Believe this, God feels your pain. He has blessed me with that gift too. I can tell when people are hurting. I can feel it inside me. That's another reason to share his love.

Let me tell you about the Holy Spirit that is forever running around inside me. Yes, this spirit is in my blood. He reaches every part of my body, mind, and soul forever guiding me on the right path. He is my gateway from this earth to Christ. He keeps my mind on the right things.

I do truly understand that things of this world mean nothing. I have everything I need. I have God, Jesus Christ, and the Holy Spirit. I have a heart flooded with love, and a mindset on God. Everything I need comes to me.

When God knows it's the right time, my love for you will always be in your heart. From this day forward, you can't get rid of it once it's there. Now your stuck with it, but it is God's love. I told you my love is God's love. I'm just one way for God to bring his gift of love to this earth, and everyone in it.

You can't see how much God's love has changed me. All you see is the changed me. You don't know the man from my B.C. life. I'm so happy that God has put you in my life. I quit asking him why. I have learned to enjoy what he does. Now there's someone to share this love with. Please open your heart. Let his love flow in. Feel the power of his love.

Say, "I love you Jesus, I love you." over and over again until the tears roll down your face. Can you really feel him? He is there with you. Now say, "I love you God. Thank you for your son, Jesus". Everything is made new through God. His love is the most beautiful thing I have ever experienced in life. It will definitely change you. You won't be the same person. The power in his love is overwhelming.

When God's love floods your heart, just hold on. You are in for a learning experience. His love so beautiful. I pray you go out and share it with others. I'm here to save people. This is what God has asked of me. He has shown me so much and given me more than I deserve. Everything I am is his. I can feel him by me everyday, his love flowing out of me everywhere I go.

I truly want this life for all. I know that I can't help everyone, but for the ones I can, I might seem pushy sometimes. That is only because I don't know how long we have left. I want you to walk through the gates to heaven. Now, I'm forever blessed because of God's love for me. I love my new life. I praise God every day for his gift, for showing me what love really is, and yes, for redeeming me.

I keep trying to help people find their way to God. So many times, people just don't get it. I'm not doing this for me. I know the life with God, all the good he does, and all the love he gives us. This is what I want to share. I help people so they can feel and know God's way and this beautiful life that he gives us.

There is nothing you can do for God not to love you. He wants all to be with him. This is why you change when you come to know God's way, you really can't come to God and not change. His Amazing Grace, love, joy, and happiness overwhelms you. It floods your heart. Next thing you know, you are changed.

I wish that everyone could understand that God only wants good for us, so stop thinking about yourself. Start thinking God's way. Life is so much better. So much good comes to us. All we have to do is give our lives to God. He gives us a new life with love that we can't understand until we know God's way. What a beautiful life it is.

The old out and the new in. Well, I was just saying this the other day when I was asked what it was like when I gave my life to God. The old life out and the new life in. Please enjoy life. It really is too short.

One thing I have learned is that sometimes we have to go through pain and hardships to become who we are. Only God knows why, but the people he puts in our lives to help us (WOW amazing). Everyone God has put in my life has helped me or I have learned something from their time in my life. Yes, even you!!!

Now, I am to help you. I have told you I'm not going anywhere. Now, I am telling you why. You are to know God's love the way I do. If you think I am such a nice person, then maybe you should have known me before. Then you wouldn't "think". You would "know". Yes I am - I'm definitely different.

What I am trying to say is, if God can take me the biggest piece of garbage and make me who I am today, imagine what he can do with you. Your heart and soul are just crying out for this kind of love. I can see it in you. I can feel it every time I'm around you. This is why I'm being pulled to you. God's love is overflowing from me. Yes, it pours on you when I am around you.

Think about this. Do you feel different when I'm around you? Do you feel more happiness and joy inside? That is God's love. Now, from the time I gave my life to God, I have never lost that happiness and joy. Yes, I have had some things that hurt me. You know this. I just had to forgive and release it - let go. Fall back into the love God gave me. You see, his love is for me, but it is in me to share with everyone I come in contact with.

This feeling when you see me, don't it put a smile on your face? Don't it put comfort in your heart? This is what I'm trying to share with you. Only god can do this. You already have some of this love in you,the love in your heart for me. Face the fact that I have told you that if you love me, you love God because my life is God's life. I am who I am because of God. To love me is to love God. God sent me to you as much as he sent you to me. It is time to stop trying to hide from him. Stop saying your not ready or that your life is too messed up or that you don't have time.

Let me tell you this. Any time is time for God. He is there to help us with all things. He is the one that can fix your life. He will crush the devil's grip on you, and as of being ready, you can never be more ready than you are right now. Jesus did not come to earth for the righteous or perfect. He came for the broken and the sinners. (Luke 5:32)

Ok, God loves you. He sent me to you and I'm not going anywhere no matter what.

(I am here for you!!!) It's in your hands. You have to want it.

The hardest part is if I have to walk away knowing that I'm taking this opportunity with me. I'm wishing I hear you say, "Wait a minute. I want what you have for me". Remember we can't make them do anything. We can just pray for them and love them.

Thank you, God, for all you do and have done. Thank you for the people you put in my life. Thank you, Lord, for all of your blessings and gifts. Most important of all, thank you for your love because without your love, we are nothing. Amen.

I was awake, but dreaming. Some call it a vision. I was looking right at the face of Jesus Christ. I opened my mouth to ask why me. Before I could speak a word, Jesus said that I belong, that I am one of his brethren while opening his arms to many tables put together as one with an army of people at them. Then he says for me to come sit at his table. He tells me to eat of his fruit.

I'm sitting, looking across the table at Jesus. I look up and down the table. Everybody there is talking and laughing. I could feel the love just pouring out of each and every one of them. Thinking that I still needed to know, I opened my mouth and only one word came out. (WHY) of why me. It went silent in a heartbeat. All that I could think of then was to write it down before I forget.

I opened my eyes and started writing. I had a feeling that I missed the message from Jesus. I closed my eyes, trying to go back to him, trying to get to that place of pure love, joy, and happiness. Nothing happened. Now, tears are coming out of my eyes. My human mind couldn't understand. That was my answer!!!

I will not ask why me again. I know there is a place at his table for me. Jesus said that I belong. Did I miss the message from Jesus? No. I see and understand it clearly now. Not only did I see the face of Jesus,but he said I am one of his brothers. He who has many, has one more. "I am all yours". JESUS

The Devils Grip

In Matthew 4 : 8–9 the devil tells Jesus that he will give him all the kingdoms of the world. If he will bow down and worship him.

So then Satan has ruled the earth for a very long time. No wonder man always does the wrong thing. After living many lifetimes of the devil's ways, it will make anyone think they are doing right when they are doing wrong.

I'm trying to figure this out. Why is it that the more I tell you, the farther you seem to drift away? Just like when I tell people the truth. They seem to run away. Well, I can't seem to wrap my mind around this. Why do people do this? Why do they run away from the truth? Does it really hurt that much? I know they say the truth hurts, but wow. Really, what I'm telling you cant hurt you.

I'm only telling you of a better life where all you do is live in the truth, where you are surrounded by love. The happiness and joy overwhelms you. Yes, this life is possible for all, even you, so please stop running away from what I'm trying to give. My words are of the way, the truth, the life. I'm only here for a short time. My hope is that these words last forever. You see, these words are the words of Christ.

Everything I write comes from God. He has done this to me. In my past life, I could never have done this. For real, I would never have been talking about God. I was not a believer then. He has done some amazingly awesome things to me. He took me out of the darkness to be one of his chosen. He gave me a life I really don't deserve.

This is why I tell everyone about this life. Believe me, if I can have this life after all I have done, just think about how much you can have. Yes, this joy is for everyone.

The love and grace is so overwhelming. Just knowing you are loved unconditionally, that all your sins are gone where you don't have to live in shame and guilt. Believe me, I was the one that not in a million years would have believed this life to be possible.

To me, God was just something made up. He was another way for someone to take your money. Now that my eyes have been opened, I know the truth, the life, and I know the way. That is with Jesus Christ, the one that man put on the cross. He still asked God to forgive us. He sacrificed his life to give us a way to God. That way is at the cross.

Yes, each and everyone of us has a cross to pick up. My question is, are you willing to give your life to God? Are you ready to live in the truth where you don't have to run away from it, where life is beautiful every second of every day? To be free from all the shame, to really know forgiveness and be able to forgive just to know true love, God's love. Yes, it is truly worth everything.

When we have the holy spirit running around in us, this is the feeling that is truly unexplainable. You know that God has control of your life. Not only can you feel it, you see it too. You see all of the stuff God does for you and to you. You start seeing beauty in everything. This is God's love at work. He truly only wants good for us, so pick up your cross. Please stop running away from the truth. Find your way with Jesus. Enjoy your new life.

Why is it that when we do something for people, they think that there are strings attached? It's because that is the grip the devil has on them. God says to love others as he loves me. People really don't get this. When I do nice things for others, they think I want something from them or that I'm expecting them to do something for me. Look, if I do something for you or give you something. It's free. There's no strings.

I never want anything back. Believe me, I get more out of giving than I could ever get from receiving. God's love has changed me. This I know. Humans just can't understand God's love. I'm really starting to believe what I was told by someone. They said I wasn't human. I'm a Christian. Can this be what is wrong in the world?

Man doesn't believe that people can do good for others. If you do good, your not human. People just can't seem to get it. There are some good people in this world. It really seems to blow their minds when you do something for them or give them something.

Don't even try to offer them stuff. That is when you get that look like you just did something wrong. And the question why would you do that for me? Tell them it's a God thing. That's when you get the, "no you can't do that," or "I won't accept it". Then, if we try to surprise them and do something without them knowing, they actually get mad at you. Why? It's because I do something for you, try to pick your spirit up, try to make your day a little brighter, put some joy in your life.

Has man really made this world believe that no one can do good, because that is what I see all the time. If I want to help you, then just enjoy it. Believe me, if God didn't know you needed it, I would not be doing it.

Now tell me this. If God says to do something, do you do it or do you wait for that voice that tells you to let them do without, that they aren't worth your help, or they can wait till they get the money for it. I know that God does not want us to think this way. God tells us to love your neighbor as you love yourself.

Do you see how messed up people are? All it is now is take, take, and take some more. People don't really know how to give. That is the word they can't understand, "give". (To freely hand over possession to someone.) There is the other word, "Free". We don't understand that one either. (without cost or payment)

I know that man has lost these words. Growing up, I was taught that nothing is free, that everything always comes with a price. Guess what, that is a lie. That's man's way of thinking. We as humans let the devil get in our heads, tell us lies that make us believe his ways.

The day that we give our lives to God, he will open our eyes to see all the lies we grew up with and believed were truth. He will give us the understanding that there is good in the world, that there are some that do good for others. Wouldn't this world be a better place if people would just care about others? Try to do something nice for someone. See how you feel.

Here's my dilemma. I know I'm the one that is to help you, I'm just not feeling you putting the effort out to do this. I told you it's a 100% commitment. I can't come over there, grab your hand, and drag you where you need to go. If you really want this life, you have to be committed to it. That means nothing gets in your way.

Nothing should be stopping you of your time with God and getting yourself clean, so when you have the guts to tell the devil no, when you want to stand up to the devil, tell Satan no. Not now, and not ever again. Tell him that you want a life with God, and mean it.

When you want out of the devil's grip, call out to God. Let the holy spirit guide you. If you need me, I'm here. I'm not going to leave you, just can't get pulled down anymore. Open your heart to God. You know what is right. I know I have told you that a life with God will not mix with the life you have. That is why he gives you a new life.

It's on you - time to pick the road you want. I really don't know what to do for you. Please help me help you. I want so bad to hold on, but can't. I feel you slipping away.

This world has a lot of evil in it. This evil tells us things like it's ok nobody will know, or I'm young let me have fun. Let me tell you, God knows. He has been fighting evil for a very long time. This enemy tries to tell us things that tempt us into believing that what we do or believe is the right thing.

Let me get in your ear a little. I actually lived with the enemy. Maybe that is my advantage. I know how he works, things he says. I've seen a lot and done even more. He is very sneaky. He will try to turn things around on you. He will make you believe that his way is right or what you are doing is wrong. The devil gets in your head, says things trying to act like God. He's trying to be god.

I'm going to be honest with you, Satan has managed to really hurt me. He has used someone that I love to do this. He is so scared to come after me himself. To use this person shows me that he is grabbing at threads.

Ok, now why I'm hurt is because of who he used. I have been trying so hard to keep this one in line. Every time I get her there, he is pulling her back. Now he has filled her full of guilt and shame. She is saying that she hates herself now. She keeps beating herself up over this. She is definitely falling into his ways. I'm trying to catch her, but her hands are not out.

Why would he hurt somebody like her to get to me? He already knows that he will never get me back, so why torture her. I know he is the king master of the lowest garbage ever made. You know, Satan, doing this hurts really bad. I only have one thing to say. It's not going to happen Satan. Get behind me. I have my God forever. I'm never going back to your ways. I will stand here and fight you any day. I have beat you once already. Yes, I have God by my side. Don't forget about Jesus and the Holy Spirit that's inside me.

See, you are defeated before you start. You know this. That is why you take the coward's way out, using people that mean a lot to me. It's pretty bad when a human has gotten so tired of you, that I'm willing to fight you. This time, I promise you that it's going to be a lot more than just beating you. I'm going to make sure that you think twice before ever going after somebody I love again.

I know what you are thinking about me. I'm not going anywhere unless God is there with me, so guess what, bring it on. When you come after me, remember. The Holy Spirit is forever living inside me. I have Jesus by my side, and God is on my other side.

Wow, what happened? Did you run away? I'm not with you anymore. I don't like you, I don't like your ways. Everything about you is all wrong. Your lies are so easy for me to see now. There's only one thing I don't understand. Why do you hurt people?

You really don't have any compassion for mankind, do you. I know everything in your world is all hurt and lies. Let me tell you this one thing, Satan. I'm not going to come back to your ways. Get it - never going to happen. Stop trying. God won. You lost "again".

Yes, everything happens for a reason. You showed me something doing this.

You showed me just how scared you really are. You know that things are changing. You can feel God moving, right? Your days have just become numbered, and you know it. Now I know that no matter what, I'm right where I belong. I'm with my God and Jesus. There truly is no greater place to be.

I have heard that the closer we get to God, the more the devil tries to get us. Yes, I listened, agreed, and believed, but really didn't understand until now. Yes, the devil is pulling everything out, trying so hard to get me back. He has tried all the old ways, but they don't work anymore, so now he's being conniving in his ways.

He's using things and people to pull me down, hurting me physically and emotionally. Truthfully, I'm here laughing at him. You see, the devil has lost. He is weak. God told me to be prepared for this, that Satan wanted me back, that he will try a lot of new things to get me.

That will never happen. Not now, and not ever again. I'm done with that life. I love my life with God, so let him keep trying. I need something to laugh about. Everything he is trying, I can tell it's him. His lies are so obvious to me now.

The physical pain, I can deal with. After all, I have lived a lifetime of it. It's the emotional pain that hurts, how Satan will use those we love just to hurt us, how he will manipulate things to his advantage. The devil doesn't care about those he's using to get to me. Yes, it hurts, but it hurts them more when they finally realize what they have done.

I can see the hurt, the pain in them. Yes, I do forgive them, but they can't understand how I can so easily. They are still caught in the ways of the world. They truly don't understand forgiveness. I know it's the evil of the world that makes people think that way. I know it's Satan showing his control. Now when I see him trying so hard to get me back, it shows me how much he is losing control.

I know he is getting mad because nothing is working. I'm here for God. The life God gave me is a beautiful gift, a true miracle, so why would I ever give it up to go back to the devil's playground. I already lived that life. It's not fun. God's life is so amazing.

It's full of love, joy, and happiness. I know that Satan will never stop trying. I also know that I'm staying in my life with God no matter what the devil throws at me. I have God, Jesus, and the Holy Spirit with me. I will not fail God has told me this. Yes, I know and believe it.

Why do some people try to get us back to the person we used to be? They can see we're doing so good. They just do things that bring our past back, putting things in our hands that shouldn't be there, but then it's not just them. We put ourselves in that position, in that place.

What is it really? "Temptations". From who, the devil? Or is it just something that we can't come to terms with. What we really want. This is where it gets tricky. Our wants and desires can really change us. It's so easy to give in to the flesh.

To do what we are so used to doing, going back to our old ways, the person we used to be, why would we want to do this. Do we not live a better life now? Why let our wants and desires cloud our judgement. It's called being human. Yes, God knows we will mess up from time to time. That is why there is a sea of forgiveness.

His mercy and grace is unending. Yes, he is always by our side, just waiting for you to ask for his help. I know I had to call out to him. Yes, I'm human too. Yes, I was just tempted with something that almost got me. Thank God for my strength and my trust in him.

I had in my hands what I know would have brought my old self back. I could feel the devil pulling on me. With God, Jesus, and the Holy Spirit in me, I turned around and laughed in the devil's face. I said, "You can't have me. Try harder next time".

God has given me eyes to see Satan's traps, his lies. This was something new to me. I never have been tempted like this, with what he used. God's love, grace and forgiveness is so much stronger than the devil's temptations.

I really can't lie. I did think about it. Then, I thought it's not what should happen. It's really not even close to what is truly wanted. You see, the enemy will pry on your weakness. He knows things about you, and he will use them. He wants me back so bad now. Trying this was very low. Years ago, I would have been all over it with both hands.

This life God has given me is so awesome. It's really amazing how he has taught me what is right because that could have went so wrong so fast. Wow, it's really hard to believe I just walked away even when I could hear, "It's not like your doing anything wrong". It's all wrong when it's not right.

God has given me a new life. I don't live like that anymore. I don't do those things anymore. I'm only here to do what God wants. Believe me, he did not want that to happen, how much I could feel the devil pulling on me. I could feel God in me saying not today. It's not going to happen.

Yes, God is in me. He is my guide, my savior, my life. I know and believe that this is my way. Now, for the devil to use this person is so wrong. This person is not really a bad person, just made some mistakes in life. Why use someone like this to try to get to me? If not for forgiveness, I would be really hurt because I still have love for this person.

The devil is the lowest of the low with all he's doing to get me. Now, the hurt that is involved. How can the enemy do this? I forgot that he doesn't care about us. He never has, and never will. I only hope that this person can get over what they have done, if they can only see that it was the devil working in them to get to me. I see it, I know it.

I can only help when they stop hurting, realize the truth, and understand that I forgive them because I know the true evil here. You see, God has told me the devil will try to get me, that he will do things I have not seen, new things.

See, God was right. It's over before it starts. The devil knows this. Why else would he try so hard to get me. He knows I'm not coming back to his side in his ways. He doesn't want to lose, but he has already lost this battle. I'm with God now. I know the way, the truth, the life.

I really do hate the way the devil did this, but I know that everything happens for a reason. I pray that this person can get out of the grip of the devil. Please, God, help them find their way back to you safely. Help them understand the hurt they are feeling now. Please show them the way. Let them experience your love.

I know that with God, I am in his light walking on the right path. Yes, I do stumble. Yes, I do fall. No matter what, God is there to help me along the way. Thank you, Lord, for your unconditional love and your understanding, and thank you for your forgiveness.

Tell me why some people can't seem to understand this. They are always saying that you can't give everything to God. They say that if you could, then you would be perfect, and they say that's impossible because a human sins everyday, but principal 3 says, to consciously choose to comment all my life and will to Christ's care.

I don't know about you, but all means everything to me, and yes, my life and will to Christ. I can honestly say that I gave all of me to God, everything. God gave me his life in exchange for mine, so why say I'm wrong and that it's impossible. I might be new at this life with God, but I know that nothing is impossible with God, so are they that misinformed.

Are they now believing the lies that are told to them, or is it that they don't have a relationship with Christ. Yes, they talk like they do. For real, if they did, then they wouldn't be saying these things. Let's talk about sinning every day. Not everyone sins everyday. What is a sin to you? Think about that. Let it roll around in your head. When you know, then come talk to me.

Answer this question. Are you sinning? If you don't know, it's a sin. Now, do you believe that all sin is the same, or is there one sin greater than another. Ok, then if we are sinning everyday, then we should be coming clean with God every night, asking for his forgiveness, praying that Jesus washes us clean with his blood again.

Now, how many times are you going to do this. Get right with God the first time, then you don't have to make up excuses for the life you want to live. When you are 100% with God, he will give you a new life. I know he gave me new life. Now, the other part is yes, as long as I stay in his light, I cannot sin.

That's just it, "in his light". The problem with that is that we are human. Yes, we do stumble, and yes, we do fall, but if we keep our faith in God and we believe always, he is right there to pick us up, and put us back in his light. The thing is, we have to look to him, ask for his help. Yes, every time we fall or stumble, just be strong enough to ask for forgiveness.

He will always love us no matter what we do, but we have to choose to go his way because the other way is not good. If you go that way, I pray that you make it back and ask Jesus to wash you clean again. Please come be a child of God, one that has a place in his house. Just look up and say, "GOD I LOVE YOU!!!" It is our love for him, not his love for us, that is in question here.

Ok God, this one thing we do, we know it's not a good thing, but we still do it. We all have different reasons for what we do. Some of us just got stuck with it because of the way we used to live. People need to know that there is true forgiveness, that you forgive no matter what. I keep telling them this. Now I know that they have to understand and believe.

Some of them think what they do is so bad that there is no forgiveness. I tell them that God says no matter what, so what is it – they can't forgive themselves. I hear you now, Lord. True forgiveness starts with forgiving yourself because we can't forgive anyone If we can't forgive ourselves.

How can we understand forgiveness if we can't truly forgive? Yes, we can say that we forgive, but until we feel it inside us and know that it is so, then it's just words. Yes, it's not just saying it. You have to feel it too. True forgiveness comes from the heart.

There is so much Grace and mercy in forgiving. Look at it this way. Jesus asked God to forgive when he was hanging on the cross. Think about what kind of love had to be in him to do that, to go through all that he went through, and still have love enough for us to ask God to forgive us.

Now, we come to this point in forgiveness. (Love). I have told you that everything God does is because of love. Now, can you see how true forgiveness is love. That's the feeling I was talking about. When you feel this grace, mercy, love, and you truly forgive, happiness, peace, joy, and freedom is your reward. What else is there.

God's love is in you. It has been from day one. It's when you open that door, it will flood you. When we become true children of God, we will start to understand God's way, how everything is separate but one. Other words without this, this, and this, you can't have_____. Get the picture?

God has made things very simple for us. Now when you think about it, it's very complex. That is why life with God is a 100% commitment. You know, God says we are forgiven, that we deserve what he gives. (Love, mercy, grace, forgiveness, freedom). He says his grace is enough. Have you truly accepted his forgiveness and all of his amazing gifts. When you truly do 100%, he will change your life.

Thank you, God, for your forgiveness of my sins, and the love you gave me so that I may understand forgiveness, and be able to give forgiveness when it is needed. Thank you for the awesome gifts you have given me and put in my life. You have truly blessed me beyond all comprehension.

Now you're showing me how people try so hard to hurt others, how they let the devil control what they do, how nothing can mean more to them then to hurt others. More than this, they think that they are in control, that what is happening is what they want.

They will try to con you into their games, where they bring you into a situation that you know is not right. How many times do you sit there and play that game with them? How long do you play until someone gets hurt? Now, are you the one that caused the hurt. If so, what does that make you, all over playing someone's game, or was it the devil's game.

See, when you know it's a bad situation, then why even get involved. Are you not strong enough to just walk away? If you have Jesus in you, your strong enough, so stop making excuses for stuff you want to do. Face the fact that you like that drama too. If you really don't like it, then ask Jesus to help you. Tell him that you know your weak.

Ask him to help you walk away. Not just from this situation, but all you know are wrong. Ask God to guide you and give you strength. Let him know that you are tired of playing the devil's game. Let him show you how some people are poison to you. Those are the ones you really need to stay away from. Just stand up and walk away. You will see that they will be the ones in disbelief.

When you do this, keep Jesus with you because the devil will come at you a lot harder next time. He really can't stand to lose a soul. That hurts him more than anything. I know this. I was his best friend. I know his ways and lies.

He keeps fighting for me. He wants me back so bad, but my life is with God. I will not go back. I can tell you this, the enemy is forever trying. He puts things in my head, temping me. It's a good thing I have broke free of his grip. I know everything the devil does is a lie.

"Wow - God just said that is why I had to live that life, so that I would stay with him, be able to finish what he has planned for me because I will have to be completely devoted, stronger than I have ever been. He said that the devil is pulling out all the stops on this. He said to be careful. Do not fall on the ways of the world. He loves me".

See, this is what I keep saying. God knows all things. Yes, he is telling me things before they happen, preparing me for them. He wants me to be ready. Everything happens for a reason. Thank you, Lord, for showing me how people lie and play with us. You see, we want to boast about what we have done or what we get, the things we buy, how we take more pride in the things of the world. We get more excited over these things than we do about Jesus or God.

Where is the Glory for God. Have we really lost our site of his love? Where is the praise for God. Why do we care about earthly things more when all praise should go to God. Yes, we are looking for that self gratification. We just put God second to so much in our lives. We will praise man's words faster, louder, and yes, with more excitement.

Do you see what this world is coming to? Satan really does have a grip on all humanity. Now do you understand? People are saying that God values things of this earth such as gold, silver, money, and the things you buy. They are saying that church is telling them this.

Yes, God values things like humans, animals, and nature. Really, God does not value possessions or money. That is Satan working in the one telling you this. The bad thing is, you believe it.

There is nothing more valuable than the human soul. Jesus said that it is harder for a rich man to get through the Gates of heaven than it is for a Camel to fit through the eye of a needle. When you understand that, then think about what you are saying, the ones you turn away for not having things are more righteous than those that carry gold or silver around. Drive BMW's, Lexus, and Cadillacs.

You see, all the money in the world can't buy you a way into heaven. You definitely can't drive there. If you read your Bible, it tells you there is only one way to heaven, through Jesus Christ or Lord. The ones you are turning away have more than you know. They have a relationship with God, Jesus and the Holy Spirit. I pray you come to realize this. Find a way to break free from the devil's grip.

People, if you don't like what I'm saying then stop reading. Don't go any further. "I don't care". Jesus said there will be ones that don't, like you. Just remember, they didn't like him first.

It seems like everyday, I hear someone disrespecting God. What is wrong with people today. How can they disrespect God and go about their day like they did nothing wrong. Are they too caught up in the world to care about God? How about how he feels and what he thinks.

Some people don't care. They view him through the eyes of the world. They don't even know what they are doing. It's just like talking when I'm playing music. They say, "Turn that off. I don't see how you can listen to that garbage". When I'm talking about God they're saying, "This is not church".

It seems like if you talk about God, people don't want to listen, but if you are talking about the devil, the things he does, they all listen. They always want to hear more. All people want to know about you is your past and what you have done wrong, so answer this.

Why did we give the devil the earth? We did this because he makes us believe his way is easier to get what we want. We all know that what we want is not what we need. It just keeps getting worse and worse. We're fading God out. That's total disrespect.

Look at it this way. God gave us life, right? So why do we blame him for things that go wrong? Yes, this world is full of evil people, ones that do a lot wrong to us and hurt us. I know this is a really hard place to go, but why disrespect God by blaming him for it. Evil people do evil things, and they will be judged for what they do.

God wants you to understand so badly. He loves you and wants good for you. If God was to take away our free will, then what would we be. We must have the right to choose the way we want in life. God wants us all to come to him, but it is up to us to make that choice. Yes, we are always going to have evil people because the devil rules the earth. We really do live in a world of evil.

It's all because of man's disrespect for God. Yes, man cusses him and says he is not real, but then they will say that the devil made them do it. They will shake their fist at God too. Yes, even at church. People are talking when service is going on. They act like praise and worship doesn't matter to them. They act like all they have to do is show up.

Now I have one thing to say to all the disrespectful people out there. If you want to be disrespectful, stay at your place. Don't bring it to church, and don't bring it to CR. Don't bring it to work, and please don't bring it around me anymore. I'm at the point now that I will say something to you.

God is the reason that I'm here today. Believe me, if I never found God, I would be dead now, so yes, he will get all my respect everyday. For those of you who disrespect God, I hope you find some respect because no matter what you do, I still love you. Yes, just because I love you doesn't mean I have to like you. I would just like to see a little respect for God, please.

We humans owe God so much more than that. I'm telling you, your day will come. Now is the perfect time to get right with God, so let's start with a little respect. I heard it can go a long way.

God, your saying to guide them until they understand how to look with their heart. Wow, you are putting so much on me now. How can I guide them if I'm not sure they want this? What about the ones that say that they want my life, then go out and do their thing after I drop them off. I really can't forget the ones that lie. We know they are lying, so then who are they lying to, themselves.

How am I to guide them? On the right path, I hear you. That is right. I can only guide them. I can show them, but can't make them go that way. The day you said I am to save people, I didn't understand. Now I do. I can't save everyone, but I can guide some to you. It's that one special someone that you want. That's why you have me here.

I'm doing all I can to help you. I'm trying really hard to keep them on the right path. You have told me that it is their choice. Now you are pushing me to help. If it's their choice, why push me? What does it mean when you say that time is running out? Is it my time, their time, or all time.

I know your not in our time, so how do I show them to look with their hearts. This is something that needs your love. We need to have your love in our hearts. How do we get your love? That I know!!! You are amazing God. Yes, I see exactly what you are saying.

I have to get them to open their hearts to you. When they do this, you will flood them with your love, change them so that they can see with their hearts. I know that is the most amazing feeling, that feeling when your love floods the heart. Everything is different, things come to life. You really see all things differently. You can see and know the lies told to us.

The best thing about it all is knowing your forgiveness. When we look through our hearts, we understand the forgiveness, how all your sins, shame and guilt are gone.

God makes all things possible. All you have to do is commit to God.

There is no more sitting on the fence. It's one way or the other. God's way or the devil's way. Get with it people. God loves all. He has so much for us, paradise in heaven, eternal life, what is the other way? Satan, lies, hurt and a lot of pain. Is that the life you want.

How can you choose that life after Jesus gave his life for us. Think about this. Could you put yourself in his place? Would you carry a cross up the hill knowing that you are to be crucified. Not only that, but you do it to take other people's sin.

It doesn't stop there. You ask God to forgive while you're hanging on the cross, to have that much love for us. We really don't deserve any of this, so why? It's because God said it is to be, so that all may have a way to him. Jesus is the way, the truth and the life. When you truly believe this with all your heart, you will find the way, then you will get the truth and new life. The plus is God's gift of love.

Please come enjoy life with God. He will pull you out of the darkness if you truly believe and ask. I know. I have been there. Now, I'm trying to guide you, but it will take God to get you out of Satan's dungen.

When you think that you have everything under control, that is when nothing is right in your life. It might seem right at the time, but believe me, you have no control.

The only thing you can do is choose to make the right choice or the wrong choice. If you really think you have things under control, you are already making the wrong choice.

When you do this, you hurt people. When you hurt people, you hurt God. Do you really think he likes to see you hurt the ones he sends to help you? Then why do you make this choice? Why lie about things when we know you are lying. Remember, God knows everything, and me, I lived that life. I know all the lies. Everything you can think of, I have already done, probably more than once.

Stop lying. Get real with yourself. You know that lying is a sin. You know that you are slapping God in the face with every lie you tell. I have asked you to tell the truth. You're not lying to me, your lying to yourself. Every time you go back to that life, and every time you pick up that drink, or drug, or whatever it is that you do, you're lying to yourself.

Why do you keep lying? You can say it is the way you were raised. That is just an excuse. It is really the devil's grip on you. I know that I have told you everything that God does is from love. No matter what he does, it all goes back to his love, his most beautiful gift to me.

I really do want you to know this love, so why do you have to hurt the ones that are trying to help you. Everything in me that is of God says that you are forgiven, that I will always be here for you, that we can work through anything, and that I love you no matter what you do. Yes, I really do feel all of this for you, it's just that I'm still human. That part of me has different feelings.

I keep trying to apply God's way to this, it's just that you make it so hard. All I want is good for you. I don't understand you. You say one thing, then do something else. It makes me feel like you really don't care. Remember God's words to me. Love as he loves That means you need to know when to let go.

You see, when you start making the wrong choices, all I can do is watch and pray, hope that one day you will finally get it. The bad thing is that you know God's way. Believe me, I have tried to help beyond what I should have. All that is left to say to you is, read 2 Peter 2:20-21

If they have escaped the corruption of the world by knowing our lord and savior Jesus Christ and are again entangled in it and are overcome, they are worse off at the end than they were at the beginning. It would have been better for them not to have known the way of righteousness than to have known it and then to turn your back on the sacred command that was passed on to them.

Jesus is the way, the truth, the life. When you walk all over God's gifts', it's just wrong, and you know it!

Yes, God knows everything about us, everything we will do and everything that's going to be done. How many are there that he has to watch over "everyone", but the problem is that he's still fighting Satan for us. Yes, Satan knows us just as well as God knows us.

Satan knows all about us. He knows our secrets, our wants, and all of our desires. He is forever trying to stop us from going God's way. Satan will do anything to keep us in his grip. He will let us have everything we desire just to stay with him. He will give us everything we want just so we don't go God's way.

Take this to heart from somebody that knows him. He's not good, he is evil. You know, this world has made it so easy for us to go Satan's way. The way of evil, call it the way of the world. That's to make it sound good to us. When we come to know God and we understand his ways, then we give our lives to him, this is when our eyes get opened.

We understand how we've been raised, and what this world has done to us, how much it's changed and it keeps changing every day. This is Satan trying to fade God out of the world. Yes, there still is a constant struggle or fight for our souls. I can tell you right now, those bad things you keep bringing up, saying, "why would God let this happen". Believe me, God didn't let it happen. That was Satan working on you.

This battle over souls, you know evil cheats. You know all this bad that happens is because one way or another, somebody's not listening to the Holy Spirit. We know the Holy Spirit tells us what is right and wrong, but the devil and his little cronies that come up here actually interrupt the way this whole battle goes. The fight for our souls, they make things happen for their benefit.

You see, the devil believes that if he can get you for this little amount of time, he'll work on you and have you forever. He forgets that we have a thing called free will. Yes, we get to choose what we want. When we actually get in touch with God, learn to understand our way of thinking, then our free will can bring us back to God. That's why we have free will to do as we ought for God.

Can you honestly say that you are 100% with Jesus Christ? This is truly something you need to think about. None of us know how long we have left on this Earth. Are we truly going to live God's way, or are you going to live the way of the world, Satan's way.

I know that I have told you before, there is only one way. That is through Jesus Christ. Please don't turn your back and go the way of the world, Satan's way. See, when people say it's okay, that's how it is, that's what they do. Those are the devil's lies made to make us think it's how the world is. We all did it right.

Just because we did, doesn't make it right. I know I was wrong in all of my BC life. Just when I was living that life, I thought I was doing right. Now that my eyes have been opened, I know I was wrong. Things that I've done, I now wish I had never done them. But God tells me it's ok. Those things are what makes me who I am today.

You see, for me, to have lived a lifetime the devil's way, I truly believe that is what makes my relationship with Christ as strong as it is. When God changed me, gave me the miracle of life, I handed my whole life over to him, everything. Believe me, I'm not looking back. Life with God is truly amazing. This life for somebody that didn't believe in him. That is truly true love. I really don't deserve this life and his love. But he says I do.

God calls me one of his own, a child of God. Yes, he knows my name and he talks to me everyday. Now you can see that I have turned around. I went from living with the devil to having a relationship with God and Jesus Christ with the Holy Spirit now living inside of me. Yes, it is possible to get away from Satan's grip.

Don't ever think because you are in Satan's world you have to stay there. I truly lived there with the devil as my ruler. I listen to his lies and I believe them. Until that day I found a little faith in God, gave him my life, all of it. He reached down into the deepest darkest pit in Satan's dungeon to pull me out, so yes, look at me. I'm living proof. There is salvation even if you are in lost in the darkness.

Please come to God. Don't let Satan win anymore. After all, it is your soul. It's so amazing how when someone is trying to do right, all the things that come up, what they think needs to be done, always stops them from doing what they had planned when really what we need is to do what God wants. Our minds don't see this. We really think that what we are doing is the right thing.

If we would just stop and think about it, we would know that it's something the devil made happen just to keep us from doing what God wanted. We will put off something that we want to do just because someone calls and says, "I need you to do this for me," or, "hey let's go do this".

We do it because they will pay us or we will have fun, but is it really fun. Now do you see what our best thinking can do, how we just let things change our lives. People, if you want a life with God, you are going to have to learn how to say no "not today". Get it!!! God can do anything. It's just our free will that gets in the way. When we start choosing things over God, we already lost. We just gave Satan power to control us.

See, it's not about what came up, it's about why you stopped what you were going to do. Truthfully, if you are going to do something for or about God, then nothing should ever stop you. I learned this the hard way. I let something stop me from doing what God wanted. When we realize what we have done, there is nothing that can make you feel worse, just knowing you let God down. That is what makes it hurt so much.

I pray that you truly know how much God really does love you because even after you do this, he still loves you and forgives you. Now you have to live with what you have done, but you have to forgive yourself.

Can you, knowing you let God down?

My question now is why do people take everything they have been given and throw it on the floor. They don't stop there. They stomp on it too as if they are trying to kill it and everything it stands for even after they see your way.

They want everything you have to offer. They just can't seem to grab it, but they don't stop there. they stomp on the ones trying to help them too. Its like they really don't care, but I know they do. The enemy has that much of a grip on them that they will crush the ones they love most. Not only on this earth, you too, God.

The enemy is sitting there, laughing at us. I want so bad to go defeat that devil, but I know that it is someone else's battle. I can't fight it for them, but I can pray and ask you to help in this battle. I will be there right by their side, praying to you and helping every step of the way.

There are so many things I have learned in the last few months. It's like you have been preparing me for this. Is this what you need me to do? Can I do this? No, I can't. I need you. I need Jesus, your son. I need the holy spirit. Yes, I understand they need to want this. They need to ask you. It is their choice to make.

Yes, I know all I can do is be there for them, pray they understand and support them on their journey, let them know that they are not alone. Yes, I understand I can never give up, love them no matter what. Lord, all of this, you have already taught me. Your love is the most powerful gift of all. Ok, Lord, I will show your love at all times. Yes, even when it hurts. I can see one thing. When I asked to learn your love, Lord. You told me to be ready. Here is another part of that. You are so amazing in all that you do. Yes, I hear you. I need to give forgiveness too. That is already in place. I will forgive them, not hold anything against them. My love for them will shine through the darkness.

Lord, please pour your grace and mercy upon them. Fill their hearts with love. Please, forgive them too. Show them the way to the light. If you want me to be here, that is where I will be. I'm standing right here. I'm not going anywhere. I believe in you, Lord. Your love floods my heart. Yes, I know. I have to share it more now than ever.

Yes, I know things are going to get hard to deal with. I know that I can turn to you. I know that you only want good for me. I hear you. Lord, I will be careful. I have you. I will not fail. I trust in you God completely. The more I grow with you, the stronger I get. Yes, God, I have been out getting an army together. When this war happens, we will win. I do have many by my side and you inside me. The enemy sees this, I know.

I can feel him trying to get at me. The thing he dont realize is, I know him. I know the tricks he tries to pull. I know the lies he will tell. I know how he gets in our head, tells us it's ok. It's just a little or it's just this one time. I know this one too. You're not strong enough. Today, I am strong enough.

I have you with me, Lord. Everything you have been teaching me comes into play here. Now, I truly understand everything you have taught me. Thank you, God, for all you have done in my life. Now, a special thank you for all you do in others' lives. You know that I love you and trust you. Nothing will pull me away from you, ever.

Lord, I will continue on my walk with you, doing all you ask of me. You made me who I am today, gave me this life. Now, I'm all yours to use as you need to. I will never stop. Thank you for the love you put in my heart. I do understand it now.

Thank you for all those that you have put in my life. They all served their purpose. I have learned from all of them. Thank you for the special ones that help guide me, and the ones I love the most.

Thank you so much for the new love you have shown me. It truly is something I did not know, a feeling that I never felt before. You truly are the God of all, Lord of lords, King of kings. Nothing can compare to you. Please, God, be with me. Help me be half as good as the ones you had teach me.

Ok, this really got me thinking. I heard someone say that they deserve God's love because they are always out doing for others. They say that they spend all their free time doing things for God, so now, God has to let them in heaven. Really, why do people think this way.

First, I know I don't deserve God's love, but he keeps pouring it in me every day. He has filled me with so much of his love that I have to go out and share it with people.

Not just people I know, but people I don't know too. This brings me to the second reason for this. I'm out doing for others. Not because I'm trying to make sure I'm going to heaven. I do for others, for them, their needs, or when God tells me too.

You see, some people try to buy their way into heaven. That really doesn't work, people. I know that I really don't deserve to go to heaven. I can never say that I'm sorry enough. Not enough to make up for all the stuff I have done in the past.

The amazing thing is that God says that stuff doesn't matter to him. It's all done and over. He has forgiven me for it. Do you see his love? He has forgiven me after everything I did, even saying there is no God. His love is so overwhelming. Try to think why, and you can't understand it.

I know that no matter what I do on this earth, good or bad, it is God who says if I go to heaven. Every single one of us will hear him say, "Well done my good and faithful servant," or, "Depart from me. I know you not".

For real, I do as God asks. I don't question what or why anymore. I know that I have questioned him before. I even let someone talk me out of doing what he asked. That hurts the most because I don't ever want to let him down again. Yes, he keeps telling me it's ok. The amazing thing is, he knew I would do just that.

He has told me that I learned the most important thing then. Yes, I did. No matter what anyone says. When God asks me, I'm doing. I will never ever not do as God asks again even if he asks me to walk all the way around the earth. I will find a way to do it because with God, all things are possible.

I do believe and I know that there is only one way to heaven. Jesus came to earth to show us the way. You can only get to the father through Jesus, so come to the cross and be washed clean by his blood.

Why are you saying that I am still the same person I was. This doesn't make sense to me. You know God took that away. How can you really say I'm the same, that I can't change that much. There is no way that I can be living a new way. You say all that stuff I did will still come back out in time.

Just stop for a minute and think about what you are saying. You tell me that you are a person of God, so what is it that you don't understand. How can you be of God and not know of new life. Look at it this way. Maybe you should read your bible more, or maybe you should revisit the cross. You might have missed something there the first time. I'm not a person that knows all about this life with Christ, but I do know what he did to me.

I don't walk around telling people lies. I really don't judge people on how I feel about them. I know we can't like everyone, but we can love them. I would never say that God can't change people, so why do you say that God could not have changed me. How can you judge me on the things I did in the past when God said that all my past is gone.

I was reborn the day I gave God my life. If you really are a person of God, you should know this, but you still want to judge me on the things I did in the past. Is there not enough proof in the bible. Did Jesus change Simon to Peter? How many times do you read about people being changed in the bible. It says it over and over many times. All it takes is a little faith.

People live with things they know are wrong. Why is it that they don't open their eyes. They just want to stay in a life that is killing them even when they have opportunities for a better life, a way out of all the hurt, all the drama, and all the pain. If you know there is a way for a better life, would you not want this, especially when you are responsible for other lives.

How can we raise our kids in an environment that is clearly not healthy. Stop and thank your kids. See and hear all. Is this how we want them to be when they grow up because if we don't stop now, that is where they are headed. I'm trying to say that it's time to take a chance. If God is with you, all will be ok.

Step out of your denial. Open your eyes and see what is in front of you. "Believe". Trust in the lord. He will not take you down the wrong path. When you have a way out, take it. Grab your new life no matter what. It will be better than the one you're stuck in now. God does amazing things. He is always there for you.

Let him show you how he can fix your problems. Come look at what is available to you. Give God control. I know it will make your life better. No matter how hard it may seem, it only gets better until it has turned into the most beautiful life you know. I'm not saying It's going to be all easy. You will have hardships, and yes, some setbacks.

I can only tell you this. If you have hope, faith, and you believe. God will never let you down. Sometimes it doesn't come when we want it to. But God tells me to enjoy the time I have and don't push. In other words, patience. It will come. God knows when we need something. Yes, he will put it there for us. It is up to us to pick it up. We have to be able to understand what God does.

We can't let every opportunity slip by. When something is right there for you, accept it. You know there is nothing perfect in this world, so stop looking at your opportunity and picking at it. So somethings are not what you want. Is this really a reason to let it go away, or is it an excuse to stay where you are, or maybe it's that you still look at things through the eyes of the world, how the world says things should be.

It's really how we were raised and what we are taught, the way man says things should be. Understand God only wants us to be happy. This is why he helps us all the time. How many times has God tried to help us. Are we really aware of what he does for us, or are our eyes closed to his hand at work. Is it that we just can't see it and walk right past it, or just turn it down.

Sometimes, my mind starts to wander. That is when the enemy pounces, putting thoughts in my head. I find myself questioning why not what I want. You do so much good for me, so why not give me what I want. That is when I just have to stop. It's God's will. After all, he knows what is best for me. I understand that what I want, if it's God's will, it will happen. Maybe not now, but when he says, I will know.

My God is so good to all, full of love and happiness. His grace cleaned us, set us free. His love gave us new life. Now, just trust in the Lord. He knows what we need and when we need it. God, I gave you my life. I will not take it back. You have shown me more happiness and joy than I've had in all of my past life. Yes, I will trust your way. I will try to understand your will and not question what you do. I will forever love you and follow your way.

You truly are everything. You know all.

Thank you Lord.

I keep hearing people say that the enemy has stolen things from us, and yes, I once had this thought myself, then I came to realize that the enemy didn't steal anything. I was weak. I let him have everything, gave him anything he wanted. I didn't know what I was doing. That's exactly what he wanted, for my eyes to be blinded to the truth, for my mind to think this is how life is, for me to enjoy his way.

He wants all of us to think his way is where we find fun and happiness, and the bad thing is that we do. He has his grip on us. We live his way, laugh about the ones that don't, then one day, hopefully, we find faith in God. We call upon him to save us, give him our life. He will pull us out of that dark place, show us the light, give us the life we should have. He will change us, our thoughts, our beliefs.

This is when we know that the life we had was not us, that God made us for a reason. We are one of his children, that each one of us are special. We are loved. Then with God, Jesus, and the Holy Spirit, we can go back and reclaim what we gave the enemy.

I'm here to tell you this is true. I have only left what I wanted to. All my bad stuff, what the enemy tempts us with, and the person I was then, that person still in the pit of darkness with all that bad stuff. Now the enemy has to put up with that person. Thank God for new life.

God's Gift

The amazing hand of God, his grace, and love. The sacrifice of Jesus on the cross. How about his forgiveness, his love. Man tortured Jesus then made him carry his cross up to Calvary hill. They nailed him to it, crucified him. He still asked God to forgive us, so how much do you really believe.

See, I know that I have been redeemed. Not only because I can feel the change, but because God tells me all the time that I am. My past, I know it's gone. Yes, God says it is, but I can hold my head up. I don't have shame and guilt in me anymore. I don't want to hurt people. I want to help them. I have love for them even after all this you say about me.

I still have love for you and I forgive you. I pray to God to forgive you and show you the way, help you understand that there really is new life through him. Hopefully, one day, you will see all that God can do. I pray that God's love gets in your heart, then your eyes will be opened to the way of new life. You will start understanding things God does.

You will see what I'm saying about shame and guilt going away, then you will realize what Jesus went through at the hands of man. He came here to teach us about God, to tell us about the way, the truth, the life, to give us a way to the father. Yes, I would love to see God's love in your heart. Let him make you a true child of God.

Then when you come to talk to me, you won't have to lie. You wont judge on past things.

You see, this life is amazing. Everything you see, everything you realize, the things you start to understand. It all changes you little by little. When your walk with God is strong, your eyes will be wide open. You see things differently and you love with God's kind of love.

This is the most awesome thing because it's a kind of love we never knew before. You just need to hold on because you will be going on a ride of your life. Yes, you will be changed. Then you will understand!!!

I see the things God does in my life. It is amazing to look at how he makes things happen just to get you to one place where he knows you should be, where he needs you to be. If you are there for someone, it is very hard not to want them to accept what is there for them. You just have to remember that they have to accept it.

You can not push anything on them. We just have to let them. If they don't, then pray that they understand. Pray that their eyes will open so that they can see what God is trying to do for them.

Here's my reality. That would be the way some people twist what I say or maybe they don't understand. My life today is to help others. Still, some I try to help, act like I'm after something. Maybe they really don't know love because to know real love, true love, they need God's love.

God's love is so beautiful. Most people never get a chance to experience true love. I know I never understood love until I was blessed by God and shown true love, his love. He changed me. I gave up everything for God. He gave me his life in exchange for mine.

Is that not true love, to give your life for someone else. What a gift for someone that did not believe. He had known all the bad i did, but after everything I had done, he still loved me enough to save me from a lifetime with the devil, and death knocking on my door.

Now, some ask me how I can stay happy when I'm alone. Yes, I am by myself in so many ways, but never alone. I have God, Jesus, and the Holy Spirit with me forever. God is forever fixing me and the things that hurt me. I'm asking God to help those that dont understand or twist my words, and the ones that say I only help to get something.

Please, God, help them and bless them. Show them love so they can see the beauty of your joy and happiness. This world would be a lot better place if people wouldn't lie, if they could learn forgiveness, but that means that they would have to be truthful. Well, I know the answer for that, Jesus.

Yes, life is so good when you give it all to him. God will restore you, give you new life. You will be redeemed. I will tell you this, the life you get will change you, make you a different person. You will have love, joy, and happiness. All the good he does for you, the gifts he gives you, you will start thinking why. Why didn't I do this before I hurt all those people and myself.

Do you really think you can handle a life like this. Well you don't have to. If you truly give everything to God, you'll have no more pain,sorrow or regrets. You'll see things through a new set of eyes. You'll understand more. The gifts God gives you opens you up. Your heart starts to pour out love for everyone. Your thinking changes for the better. Now, you have a life that matters.

Hold on because God is just getting started. Every bit of this is yours. Just ask him for this life. Give him your life. It really is his life in exchange for yours. He will take your old life and give you his life. Where you are loved, you have a reason to live. You have a meaning and a purpose.

For real, you are just getting the life God made you for, and you get his reason for you. Yes, everyone has a reason, something God made you for. Think about this, I could never write like this before I came to God. At first, God told me to go save people. Then, he showed me his power. Now, he is the one doing the writing not me.

Believe this people. God wants all to come and know his way. He really doesn't want to lose anyone. We are all his children. It really is not hard to love him the way he should be because he loves us with all his love. Even when we don't love him.

Please let God know how you feel about him. Tell him he is loved!!!

Ok, everything I write about when I think back to that old life, I didn't get it either. Wow, it's so amazing how God changes the way we think. When he says we will have a new life, believe me it's true. We get a life we never dreamed about. The dreams I had of a better life can't compare, so then why did I live like that.

I really didn't know hope or faith. To tell the truth, I didn't want to. I thought I was happy with the life I had when I truly didn't know happiness. My life was so empty. Now that I know God, my life has changed. "All of it!" I can see where I never could before. My life is full of happiness and joy now. I know it's all because of God's love. This is why I wish everyone could have a life with God.

If he can change the worst piece of garbage human on this earth, think what he can do with you. My whole life before Christ was a waste. I did nothing but play in the devil's back yard, listened to his lies and believed his stories, did everything he asked or suggested. I let him be the lord of my life. When I did this, that life was not worth anything.

It's amazing how he can turn things around on you, make you believe everything he wants you to. The bad thing is, we just let him do anything he wants just so we can stay in that life with all the things it brings. The stuff we start saying we miss in life, all comes out of this messed up life. Where we don't live, we just exist.

God knew the way I gave my life to the devil, the way that I would listen to him just like he is the lord of the world. All I can say is thank God for this life he gave me.

This gift is a true miracle, to have the love, forgiveness, to pull me out of the devils lifestyle, to totally redeem me over night. Yes, I still had to work on things.

God took an unbeliever like me, someone that told people there is no God, and turned me into who I am today. He turned me into someone that praises God all day every day, that believes he can do all things, knows his power, understands things he does. How he works things out for the better, how he puts people in our lives, shows that he has reasons for everything he does.

When you can understand his hand at work, is when you start to see the awesomeness of God. You understand how his grace and love works, how he pours his grace over you, then floods your heart with love, his love.

Now for his forgiveness. It doesn't matter to him what you have done, how many sins you have committed. He doesn't keep count. All sins are gone. You can't change the past, so don't live in the past. (God doesn't.) Live for the day! Go out and do good for someone. See how you feel.

God loves you more than you could ever imagine. He has shown me this love. Has blessed me beyond measure, his life in exchange for mine. What a gift. Really, he had to give me new life. I gave the old one to the devil, so the only way to keep this gift was to have a new life.

He cleaned me completely-he had to so that I would see how beautiful this life is. So I would stay in the walk with God. He truly knows everything. If one little thing was not right, the way he wanted it to be, I wouldn't be here writing this now. The love he has for me is overwhelming.

I need God in my life everyday. This is why I listen to my music, the Holy spirit just dancing around inside me more and more with every song I play. It's funny how you can feel him inside you. What is better than that is to feel his power in your hands. I know the things he does through me. It's truly indescribable. This is why he is God.

He took me.

A man of the enemy turned me into a man of God over night. (amazing) HOW IS THIS POSSIBLE. JUST A LITTLE FAITH!!!

WITH HOPE, TRUST, AND LOVE JUST BELIEVE WITH YOUR WHOLE HEART THAT JESUS DIED ON THE CROSS FOR US, THAT WE ARE WASHED CLEAN BY HIS BLOOD.

HE GIVES US LIFE WITH NO MORE SIN, NO MORE SHAME, NO MORE GUILT, NO MORE PAIN.

Know this, everything God does comes back to his love. When I started learning his love, that is when I found out. What man believes to be love is so far off of the true meaning. I really never understood this. I thought I knew love.

I want you to understand this for me. God gave me his love, told me I had to share it with others, that I had to love like he does, to love others as God loves me. I really try to do this. Believe me, it is hard. To love someone more than anything, to be able to give my life for others, that is the kind of love that is in me now.

I always thought that I knew what love was until God showed me real true love. I love the life I have now, but I would give it up in a heartbeat to save someone else. This is the love that has flooded my heart. I'm so happy that he has chosen you to be one of the people in my life.

Please understand the word, love. God's way, and it's true meaning — The act of caring and giving to someone else. Having someone's interest and wellbeing as a priority in your life, to truly love is a very selfless act, just understand that it's God's way. You see, I love many people.

When I said that I wanted to know all about God's love and grace, his mercy, forgiveness, everything he does. It's amazing how he shows me things all the time, how he can use people to help me understand what he is trying to show me. His love is overwhelming, all the happiness and joy, but then there is hurt, pain, and emptiness too. Let me say, I was not ready for this. I'm so happy that god is by my side always. I can see how some people can lose faith here.

To know God's love is to know all of this. I love God more than anything. I will never lose my faith. I know he is by my side throughout all my life now. Everything I go through, he is there. I asked to know all of his love. Yes, he is showing me. I'm learning more each day.

I know all he shows me is for a reason. I know he is walking me through it step by step. I know I will never know all of his love, not unless I was to give my life for others. You see, that is the biggest sacrifice which is real true love. This hurt, pain, and emptiness, I know it is part of what he is showing me. It's more for me to learn. I know he will fill this part of my heart again.

To truly know love, you have to know the hurt that goes with it. God, you truly know when to show me things. If my walk with you was not as strong as it is, I can see faith leaving, but my faith just keeps getting stronger every day.

I want so much to grow with you, to share all you do for me, to help others come to know you because you are a good father. You only want good for us. Yes, I have learned that when we ask for things, be ready for all aspects of it good and bad, but you only give us what we can handle at that time. Even if it hurts, we have to learn from it. Don't dwell on it. Let go and trust in the lord. All things will be made good as long as we believe and stay with you.

Thank you, Lord, for giving me the opportunity to know more of your love and for showing me that everything you do has a reason even if it hurts us. We just have to rely on you to get us through. We know you can and will, just trust you that everything comes together. We sure can't do it on our own. Thank you for all the stuff you do for us, all the people you put in our lives, and everything you teach us. You only make me stronger. Thank you Lord.

Where does this feeling inside come from? Only God could have made me feel this way. He took me from where I was to where I am today. He does so much for me. He keeps putting people in my life to help me. I do believe that some are angels, some come and go quickly, some stay around, but I learn something from all of them.

Is this how we should view our lives. Stop and look at everything that has happened in life. Know that it is God's work. He puts people there to help us. When we walk with God, his love will show through us. Then, all things are possible. This love God puts in you, it's made to be shared with others. God's love is for all.

Never think that just because you have God's love, you are ok. You must share his love. That is when it starts growing in you. The more you share, the more you get. Then, you start to understand God's love. Never hold onto it. Give it away.

I'm living proof. The more you give away the more he gives you. It's ok if you give it to people that dont understand or believe. When they feel the love in their hearts, then they will start asking questions. We can talk to them tell them about God and all the good he does for you. That's when God comes in and starts his work. You see, God's love is made for everyone.

No matter what we do, nothing can compare to God's love for us. We really need to go out and spread God's word and love to all people, everyone we come in contact with. The day we can love all the same, that is the most amazing thing. It is how God wants us to be. Just think if all people loved like God tells us to, what would this world be like then.

I choose to keep giving his love away and forgiving those that do wrong to me. My wish is for all to know God's love.

Something amazing happened to me the other day. Someone told me that I had a special glow about me, that when they are around me, they just want to smile. That is God working through me, his love pouring out. That is the total awesomeness of God. It's his love, his grace.

We know we have it, but when someone else tells us, that is beyond all measures. Just to know his light shines in you, his love and grace flows from you like an unstoppable river, that you really are walking and talking his way.

When other people can see it, your doing something right. The Holy Spirit is so alive in you. You actually feel his hand on yours. He is showing you things, talking to you. Don't miss out on his gifts. Open your eyes and listen. God's will is happening right now. He knows what you are doing.

Walk and talk his way. Let his light shine from you too. I will always let his light shine from me. I want the whole world to see it, the light of Jesus shining so bright in me, his love pouring out of me onto others. Open their eyes Jesus. Let them see you in me.

Let them feel your love, touch their hearts, overwhelm them, make them see how life is when we walk with you. Change their hearts so the Holy Spirit can change their thinking. If we are true to ourselves and to God, we can turn our lives over. We can be reborn new life. We have to want it more than anything, not trying to hold on to anything. Give complete control to God. The mercy, grace, forgiveness, and his love overwhelms you.

It falls on you, washing you clean, fills your heart until the love flows out showing everyone you have been changed. The best part is that you can feel the change. You feel the love, joy, and happiness. You really can't stop smiling. God starts changing you into the person he made you to be. You find out what you thought was life was nothing but you wasting time.

If you really love your life with God, then you wish that you had done this a long time ago, but then, would we be the same people we are today. I know that my life before Christ is what made me who I am today. Everything I went through was all for a reason.

God knows what he is doing. He knows how strong my faith is today. He knows all my sin and still chose me, calls me one of his chosen, works through me for so much good, shows people that love really does matter. His love pours out of me everyday.

I have found a new home, somewhere I will never leave. My father is always there for me. He always has arms open wide. He tells me to come and rest. His love is so unexplainable. It is just where I will live the rest of my days.

It is so amazing how you can know all the stuff I have done in the past and still love me. Not only do you love me, you forgive me too. Tell me it's done and over with, washed clean, never to be held over me again.

So if this is God's way, then what is wrong with this world today. All anyone wants to do is hold your past over you. Try to buy a car, they want to look at your past. Try to rent a place, same thing. Even a doctor looks at your past.

Now, I found people doing online search on me, so why is it that we don't believe that some can change. Are we that lost from what God wanted? Has this world slowly taught us this to never trust anyone that has done wrong in their life. The only people these days that trust are people of God. So what does that tell you.

God is good to all. Listen, what goes on in this world has no effect on me. I really don't care if they are checking on my past. If that is what they want to go by, then it is their loss. The only thing I care about is my walk with God, staying in his light. The people that don't want anything to do with me because of my past, I pray one day you see the ways of this wrong.

This world has lost its grip on me. Anything of this world is just that, of this world. You can't take it with you, but I do have one thing I can take with me. I can take God's love. We all know it's not of this world, but I did get it here.

I have learned a lot from God. I know that nothing in this world can pull me away from God. He is the only way, the only truth, the only life. I can't believe sometimes that God chose me. Even after he tells me, I'm still in awe about it. Yes, I'm one of his chosen. Wow, knowing this changes my way of thinking.

How could the lord of all want me? That is what he keeps telling me, that he redeemed me to do what he needs me for. That is awesome. God has a plan for me that's better than anything in this world or anyone in it can say. I don't know what I'm doing.

Sometimes, I feel so different than everyone. Am I missing something? Should I feel special, because I do! Has God given me a gift that no one else has? I really don't have any problems. I keep doing what God wants me to do.

Life is so great, then I hear that there has to be something your holding on to. Really, I gave my life to God. Why would I try to hold on to anything from my past? I was given a new life. How much do you not understand about new? I completely started over. Nothing of my past is worth my time in this life. What I have done God knows and forgave me for it. Who else do I need to prove this to?

I am changed. Only God could have done this. I completely gave my life to him, not trying to hold on to anything. He gave me his gift of new life. I am telling you, the person I was is gone with all the garbage that he has done.

Why do people keep trying to get me tied up in my past? I live for the day I get to go home. Hopefully I will hear, "Well done good and faithful servant". Leave my past where it belongs. I am walking with God, nothing else matters. Keep moving forward, not backwards. Trust me, God knows all.

He still loves me.

What else is there that I need?

(NOTHING).

Some days, we need to be strong enough for others. When we need strength, we turn to what we think can help us. Sometimes what we think is help, ends up hurting us. We should remember that God is there for us, even in times we feel hopeless. He is right by our sides. We should open our hearts to him. He will fill our hearts with his love. Then God's love will open our hearts to others.

When we love God and ourselves, loving others will be made easy. Sometimes we try to help so much we don't think about love. Remember, without love we are nothing. God says to love others "AS HE LOVES". That is a lot of love. To really be able to do this, we first have to know God's love. When we can feel it pour out of us, the joy, the happiness, the Holy Spirit running wild in us, this is God's love. It is forever.

Stop. Ask yourself, have I turned it all over to God?

Does God control my life and my days? Think about this. Is God not everything? Then why are we trying to keep him from guiding us when he made us?

I walk in his light everyday. When I step out or stumble, he is right there with his hand out to me, just waiting for me to reach up to him. Then, he pulls me back into his light.

Thank you for all your love God.

I am yours.

When we live our lives doing the wrong things, we find ourselves 10st in the darkness, walking around, trying to find a way out. When we don't find a way out, we just tell ourselves that this is how life is until we believe it can't change, so we are stuck in the pit forever. I know I have been there for a long time. I found a way out, thanks to one man that showed me the way to our Lord Jesus Christ.

Thank you so much Bill. Through you, God poured his love into my heart. Then, he reached down and pulled me out of the darkness into the light. He did it in a way that all the bad stuff was left in the pit to rot. He gave me a miracle, a new life. I'm living clean and I'm happy every day. I just ask God to guide me through the day and it's beautiful.

God's grace is truly beautiful and his love is unfailing. I never thought I could ever get a gift like this. The Holy spirit runs through me. Now, it's a life that I could never ask for. When I turned my life over to God, he made me a new person. I will never throw this gift away. Let's say what it really is, a miracle away.

I will keep the Lord, Jesus Christ, in me. I will stay clean. I will not fail. I don't know why you saved someone like me. You have your reasons for everything you do.

Yes, now I am a child of God.

I truly believe that Jesus Christ died on the cross for me. Now that I believe this, I can never go back to that old life. Yes, I tried to live the way I thought was right. For real, but now I know that it's the way the devil wanted me to live. I know I can never thank God enough for pulling me out of Satan's dungen and giving me this new life.

This feeling, this way of life, it's so amazing. I want so much to be able to show other people this life. I try and try to help guide people. I need to find that one thing inside me that's going to make it possible for me to connect with all these people and show them this life of God. I know they can see it in me, especially the ones that know me from the past.

To actually live this life, I wish it for everybody. Yes, there are those that run away. There are even ones that'll try to hide. How about the ones that try to play the game riding the fence. Let me tell you, I've seen a lot of people that don't understand.

Some don't want to understand. They're still stuck in the lies this world tells us. Those lies tell us that we can do anything we want and that we can live anyway we want. When, for real, there is only one way to live. That is in the truth of life that God made you for.

You see, we all have a purpose. If we choose to fulfill our purpose, then we have a beautiful life. If we choose to live our life in the lies of the world, living the way the devil wants us to, how can we call ourselves a child of God?

I see people struggling with their own identities. They don't know who they are. They are lost in the world. This is how messed up man has made this world, letting Satan rule and making up lies for us to live by, tell us it's okay to be like that. "Everybody's doing it". Or how about this one, "Nobody will know". This lie, it's like on top of them all. Love whoever we want. Forget about the rest of the world. Wow, that was hard for me to put that sentence in here, but these are lies we live by.

When we know the truth, God's truth, it changes us. His love pours from us, we are reborn, we become children of God. This is when we realize all the lies we have been living. We understand God loves all of us, even the ones that don't believe.

I can look back at my past. I understand all the times God was there helping me. God, I can never thank you enough for this life. I don't deserve it. You poured your love into me and you gave me a new life. I'll never understand why. How is it you can take the biggest piece of garbage, this worthless human, and change me overnight into one of your children, someone that has a purpose in life.

Not only do I enjoy life, now it's full of happiness. There is nothing of this world that could have done this to me. I have heard that it would take a miracle to wash me clean. Well, it took Jesus's blood to wash me clean. The miracle was the life he so freely gave me when I gave him mine. So yes, God does love us all.

I was the worst of the worst. I didn't care about God, I didn't believe, and it was okay with me. Want to know who did care? "God cared." He has always been by my side. Everyday he is pouring his love in me. The biggest thing is knowing about their sacrifice.

God sacrificed his only son for us humans. Jesus sacrificed his life to give us a way to God. When you truly know and understand this, things in your life will change. You start to understand God's will. Yes, it may not be what we want, but it is what has to be. So now, if you love God above all, are you willing to sacrifice your life for God and Jesus, or do you believe that you're better than they are?

God is my strength. To him I give all, never holding anything back. He tells me to take my new life and enjoy it. I do what he wants me to. This is why I have his love flooding my heart every day. Yes, I freely laid my life down to him. (Everything). God has given me the power to do that. God gave me the power to pick up my life too.

Now I can enjoy life his way, a life of freedom, happiness, and joy. It's such a beautiful life, where you know true forgiveness. You are flooded with God's love. His Mercy and Grace has been poured over you. Life as you know it has been changed. You are given a new life. Yes, one more of his many gifts he has for you.

Understand, the most powerful gift God has given you is his love. For real, we could have all the faith, belief, wisdom, and knowledge, but without love, we are nothing. God's love is given to us to go out and share with others. Yes, we are to hold on to it, but we are to give it too. The more we give, the more we get.

You want to know a little about God's love? God's Definition of Love:

If I talk a lot about God, the Bible, and Church, but I fail to ask about other people's needs, I'm simply making a lot of empty religious noise.

If I graduate from theological seminary, and know all the answers to questions you'll never even think of asking, I'm nothing. If I have all the degrees to prove it, and if I say I believe in God with all my heart, soul, and strength, claiming to have incredible answers to my prayers, but I fail to take the time to find out what makes others laugh and cry, I'm nothing.

If I sell an extra car and some of my books to raise money for poor starving kids somewhere, and I give my life for God's service and burn out after pouring everything I have into the work, but do it all without ever once caring about the people, the real hurting people, the moms and dads and sons and daughters and orphans and widows and the lonely and forgotten my energy is wasted, and so is my life.

If I pour my life into the Kingdom but forget to love those here on earth, my energy is wasted, and so is my life.

Here is what love is like, genuine love, God's kind of love. It's patient. It can wait.

It helps others, even if they never find out who assisted them. Love doesn't look for greener pastures. Love doesn't boast. It doesn't try to build itself up to be something it isn't.

Love doesn't act in a loose, immoral way. It doesn't seek to take, but it willingly gives. Love doesn't lose its temper. It doesn't keep changing its mind. Love doesn't think about how difficult the other person is, and certainly doesn't think of how it could get back at someone. Love is grieved deeply over the evil in this world, but it rejoices over truth.

Love comes and sits with you when you're feeling down and finds out what is wrong. It empathizes with you and believes in you. Love knows you'll come through just as God planned, and love carries on to the end. It doesn't give up, quit, diminish, or go home.

Love perseveres, even when everything goes wrong, the feelings leave, and the other person doesn't seem as special anymore. Love succeeds 100 percent of the time.

That, my friend, is what genuine love is.

4 Love is patient and kind. Love is not jealous or boastful or proud 5 or rude. It does not demand its own way. It is not irritable, and it keeps no record of being wronged. 6 It does not rejoice about injustice but rejoices whenever the truth wins out. 7

Love never gives up, never loses faith, is always hopeful, and endures through every circumstance.

Three things will last forever. Faith, hope, and love. The greatest of these is love.

So has man become too proud to understand these words? Truthfully, the lies we have been taught growing up go against these things. The things we do go against his love too like how we delight ourselves in the evil ways. We know it's wrong, but we still do it. So why do what you know is wrong? Some say it's easier than trying to get clean. Ok, yes, you go through a few hard days getting clean, but the reward is so worth it.

God will help you. He will guide you. He's right there by your side through it all. The life you're given is so much easier to live. You actually enjoy life, you have things, you start living in the truth, and your eyes are open to a whole New world. Yes, I see God in everything. He is everywhere.

My God is an awesome God. When you get God in you, never stop learning his words. Never think you are good where you are or with what you know. I do everything I can to stay with God all day, every day. I'm always trying to learn more about him and his way.

Try this for a day. Try to learn all you can about God's love. Believe me, it's a never-ending journey. I'm still learning more about his love. The love God has for us, the love Jesus has for us, it's in every one of us. We have just been taught or chosen not to use it. Until we give our life to God, and open that door to let his love flow in us, we know not love. (True love)

The big picture, where do you belong?

I know that I stopped looking a while back. I now enjoy life. It comes at me daily. I have learned that to enjoy my days, I have to let God handle everything. I don't expect anything, and I'm not waiting for stuff to happen. When things happen, I can see God's hands working.

You know that good or bad things are going to happen, to understand that God has all things no matter what. Then you start to see that it don't matter. What is meant to be will be. If we like it or not, it's God's will. To understand he knows all, that is amazing. We just have to be ok with everything he does.

Believe me, God only wants good for us. He never wants to hurt us, but some things do hurt, and he knows it. Those things that hurt are the ones that have to be done. Sometimes for others, sometimes for us. Just trust in God. He is our strength, our guide, our power, our life, and our love.

The day we can be ok with all that God does is the day we really know about God's love. I know that I'm still learning his love. It has got to be the most incredible thing I've tried to learn. The joy and happiness that is in his love is so overwhelming. You can lose yourself in his love. It's the most beautiful thing to ever touch my heart. Well it actually flooded my heart. It's a totally indescribable feeling, so unexplainable.

God's love just leaves you in awe. It is definitely something you have to experience. To know what I'm trying to tell you, it grabs your heart, changes you. You will definitely be different when God's love gets in your heart.

If God made us, and he loves us unconditionally, why do so many run away. They're unaware of their salvation. How about the ones that don't know and are so scared to find out. What are you really scared of?

Truth, love, happiness, joy.

God, you know exactly what we need and when we need it.

I do understand that things have to be done no matter what.

Through all the hurts and joy, I'm with you all the way. I know your way is the right way, the best for all.

You are always good to me even in the bad times. I can still find you. Yes, you know when I find you, I can't help but smile. You alone make my bad days good. Thank you, Lord. My love is your love. You know all.

One day in our lives, we will come to realize that what we want is not what we need. So many times we don't think about how our wants and desires make us choose things that we don't need, things that are not good for us, but do we really care? No. Then, we don't think we have what it takes to fix our lives. This is when we need to find time for God.

Come to the understanding that only with God can we fix what is so broken in us, what makes us keep doing the same thing over and over. God's grace is all powerful. Nothing can compare. When you give him your life, he gives you love. This love is what will change you forever.

After your heart gets filled, the love keeps coming until it is flowing out of you like a flood that you can't control. It overwhelms you. That is when you realize you have been changed by God and understand only God could have done this to you, the gift of a beautiful new life, one that gives you love for everyone, everything. Wow, I really don't deserve such a beautiful gift as this. "why", how do you love me so.

So now people, it's time for you to pick up your cross, lay your sins at his feet. He has forgiven you, you're clean, you're free. That old life is gone. It's time to enjoy your new life with God, Jesus, and the Holy Spirit. You are a child of God. Come enjoy your place at his table. His love conquers all. Love him more than you love anyone. He is true unfailing love forever. No matter what he is always there for you.

Remember, he knows everything you have done and everything you will do. The best thing is he still wants you enough to leave the 99 for you. His love surpasses anything the human brain can comprehend. You are one of his chosen. Now do you understand.

God loves you!!!

1 JOHN : 3 says it best

See what great love the Father has lavished on us, that we should be called children of God! And that is what we are! The reason the world does not know us is that it did not know him. 2 Dear friends, now we are children of God, and what we will be has not yet been made known. But we know that when Christ appears,[a] we shall be like him, for we shall see him as he is. 3 All who have this hope in him purify themselves, just as he is pure. 4 Everyone who sins breaks the law; in fact, sin is lawlessness. 5 But you know that he appeared so that he might take away our sins. And in him is no sin. 6 No one who lives in him keeps on sinning. No one who continues to sin has either seen him or known him.

7 Dear children, do not let anyone lead you astray. The one who does what is right is righteous, just as he is righteous. 8 The one who does what is sinful is of the devil, because the devil has been sinning from the beginning. The reason the Son of God appeared was to destroy the devil's work. 9 No one who is born of God will continue to sin, because God's seed remains in them; they cannot go on sinning, because they have been born of God. 10 This is how we know who the children of God are and who the children of the devil are: Anyone who does not do what is right is not God's child, nor is anyone who does not love their brother and sister.

More on Love and Hatred

11 For this is the message you heard from the beginning: We should love one another. 12 Do not be like Cain, who belonged to the evil one and murdered his brother. And why did he murder him? Because his own actions were evil and his brother's were righteous. 13 Do not be surprised, my brothers and sisters,[b] if the world hates you. 14 We know that we have passed from death to life, because we love each other. Anyone who does not love remains in death. 15 Anyone who hates a brother or sister is a murderer, and you know that no murderer has eternal life residing in him.

16 This is how we know what love is: Jesus Christ laid down his life for us. And we ought to lay down our lives for our brothers and sisters. 17 If anyone has material possessions and sees a brother or sister in need but has no pity on them, how can the love of God be in that person? 18 Dear children, let us not love with words or speech but with actions and in truth.

19 This is how we know that we belong to the truth and how we set our hearts at rest in his presence: 20 If our hearts condemn us, we know that God is greater than our hearts, and he knows everything. 21 Dear friends, if our hearts do not condemn us, we have confidence before God 22 and receive from him anything we ask, because we keep his commands and do what pleases him. 23 And this is his command: to believe in the name of his Son, Jesus Christ, and to love one another as he commanded us. 24 The one who keeps God's commands lives in him, and he in them. And this is how we know that he lives in aus: We know it by the Spirit he gave us.

New understanding

Well, are you listening to people telling you don't do that, even when God is saying to do it. You of little faith. Yes Lord, I have done these things myself, listening to people digging up dirt. Whatever convinces us to not go through with it. Now, when you have faith in God, do you really think you should do these things. No if you have faith then you will trust him completely.

Look, I stopped listening to others. Especially when what they are saying is going against God and what he tells me. I have let someone talk me out of what God wanted me to do before. That is the worst feeling imaginable, to know that you let God down, that you let someone break your faith in him. Honestly I have people telling me not to print my book. Mainly because I don't have the money it takes to have it done.

They are saying all kinds of things like Christian books don't sell as good as others. You really don't know if you will sell any at all, but you know what God knows. He is the one telling me to do the book. He had me writing it for two years. Then for some reason, he tells me to put it together his way. God actually guided me in this. It was God that showed me the publisher.

Look, we know if God wants something done, it's going to happen. Yes, I know God is doing this. Everything's just falling in place. That's exactly how things work when God is in control. I know God's will. He's going to provide a way. This has to be done.

This is who I am today. The person from before, not a chance this would happen.

Thank you, Lord, for showing me mercy when I was at my lowest. Thank you for your grace and your never-ending powerful love. You really are first in my life. No matter what, I will always love you. I promise to never lose faith again.

It's really upsetting to me when the enemy uses our love against us. He will put his lies in our mind through our thoughts or ideas. Then, we start to question what is good in us, the love we have for others. Yes, sometimes even our love for God. He is sneaky and conniving. He's always trying to get to us.

If we stop and think about our feelings and the ones involved and the situation, we can see it's not good. Then we know it's not of God. Most of us don't think about things. We just act on what we believe to be right. Stop doing what we want. Do what God wants.

You can believe God only wants good for us. The outcome of any situation is the proof of that. Can you really thank God for everything that happens in your life. Just because we don't like some things he does, at that time it is what has to be, God knows best for us.

He would never do harm to us, never put bad thoughts in our head. Thank you, God, for your blessings. Even if I don't understand them at the time you give them. My love will always be with you because I know it's your love inside me. THANK YOU!!!

If we really live this way for his words, nothing can harm us, but we have to be 100% in him. I know and try every day to follow his ways. When I really understand I need help, he is there guiding me, fixing me, or showing me the way.

I truly believe in God with all I am. I give everything to him. When we do that, it changes us inside. We know that we can never go backwards because we are not only his child. We are his chosen. We know he has placed the crown upon our heads.

When he makes it known to us, it's unexplainable. I know when I saw it with my own eyes, I just said God's hand at work. You see, all the power of this earth, all the money can't defeat God or his plain. A true chosen child of God. Is truly lifted higher than most. As it says in Psalm 112:8,

Their hearts are secure, they will have no fear; in the end they will look in triumph on their foes.

My God is true to his words. You see, I have seen the power and money get tossed aside like it's nothing. Believe this one thing – with God, all things are possible. Now, really live by that knowing it's true with all your heart. Then understand, trust not just the way of man.

You have to know trust without borders, really trust. Does God have to earn your trust? I know that my trust is stronger than life. Yes, my life is his because of his love. That is what makes my trust so strong, "His love".

I was talking to God. You know, I do fear something. Well as of a minute ago, I did fear. God has done to me what he is always doing, fixing me, explaining where I'm letting myself ahead of him.

You see, I feared losing Brittany. Yes, she is important to my life. God told me this, but he says she is very special to him. When I hear him say that, it makes me think back. Now about two years ago, God told me he was sending an angel to help me. Truthfully, that's around the time I met Brittany.

I truly believe with all my heart that my angel is Brittany. Her beauty, her heart, everything about her, the way he has used her to help me more than once. Then, what happened yesterday when I dropped her off. I haven't said anything to anyone mainly because I can't explain it.

When she turned around and looked at me to say bye, I saw something that left me speechless. I'm getting off track. See, God has used Brittany again to teach me something. He just revealed this to me in our conversation. He told me to think about the love I have for her. Then he said to explain it to him. Well, I can't really. I would give my life for her in a second without hesitation. I would spend the rest of eternity in the devils playground for her. My love for her will never die or leave. No matter what, I'm always going to be here for her.

Then, he said what you feel for her. Imagine that 100 times stronger. From day one, before you were born. That's the amount of love God had for me. That made me cry, to know he loved me that much. You see, the love I have for Brittany, I have never felt a love like this.

Now, I know what God is doing to me. He is still showing me his love. When you ask for something, he does it. Now knowing this, I understand because with just the love I have for Brittany, I would search Satan's dungen i would climb down in the darkest pit there to find her. I would give my life to my old buddy Satan forever just to get her out of there.

It makes me think about the love God truly has for us. He actually loved me that much when I hated him, when I told people there was no God. So now, I know his reason for this. I also know Brittany will be in my life for the rest of my days. He said she is here to stay and I trust him completely.

When we stop and think about the people God puts in our lives, it's truly amazing how he knows when to have certain people come in or out of your life. He will remove the ones when they can not help you anymore. The truly amazing thing is when he leaves certain people in your life. Especially when they mean so much to you, like Brittany, his true gift to me. The bond and love is amazing. See, he does know everything we need in life.

Matthew 24: 36 says that no one knows the day or hour for the return of the Messiah. Not the angels, not even the son. It says only the father knows, so I'm stuck on this one. They say the son and father are one. If this is true then the son would know the day and time of his return.

So now God, please help me with this one. Yes, I understand Jesus is Jesus.

You are you.

The Holy Spirit is the Holy Spirit.

Only your spirits are the same. I understand you gave your spirit to him when he was born, the same way you give us your spirit when we are reborn. Just because we are one with you doesn't mean we know everything you know. See how amazing you are. I ask and you tell me.

You are so fast to give me your wisdom and knowledge. Yes, you always answer me. Sometimes it's not what I wanted, but still, you know what is best and I will not question your will. No matter what, I know what has to be will be. Thank you Lord.

Yes, I know I'm not where I belong. God, I know you created the world. You created man to live here and take care of your creation, but all man has done is destroy. I look at this world. I know that I was made to live here. Everything tells me this. The way this Earth works, all together as one. We really take your work for granted.

Then, us humans gave control to the devil. We would rather live his way, listening and living his lies. Humans destroy everything they touch even when it's something we really want. Yes, for real God, I know I'm not where I belong. I know I belong with you.

See, that's where it all got messed up. You used to walk and talk here. Now, this world is so full of sin. It's completely unclean. Everyone on the earth has sinned. You saw this a long time ago. Why is it that it's easier in our head to live that way. When we stop living that way, we can see it was a hard life, one that we made for ourselves.

All throughout that life, I tried to blame others or make up reasons why life was like that. Now, I want all to see this life. It truly is an easy life to live. You wake up in the morning and let God guide you. It's so amazing when you actually do this, just knowing God has everything. He knows what you need.

Us humans have to stop living the way of the world, "the devil's way". We try to blame God for what doesn't go right in life. Some of this is just evil people that like to hurt others for their pleasure. Then, some is just the way we live, what we want, and how we treat others. We need to stop thinking the way we do.

Change your heart and your mind will change too. Look at this world through God's eyes. There is a lot of hurt here. We humans caused it. Now, let's come together and fix this beautiful creation. That is everything!!! The earth, nature, animals, and people. Let's give this world back to God. I just want to go home!!!

One day, we will all see the light. Our eyes will be opened. Those of you that know this, that have been through this, God has put you here for a reason. You see and understand what I'm saying. We are to spread his words, to let others know about his love.

I keep trying to do this everyday. It just seems like the more I try, the more the devil gets in the way. He is forever throwing something out, trying to stop what I'm bringing out in someone. I have come to realize God's love is in all of us. We just have to open the door and let it flow.

Let me tell you something else too. When the devil does this, he is trying to get in my head too, telling me I did something wrong. He's trying to tell me that it's my fault they are choosing what they are, that I was pushing them. See, I know these lies. I really have to stop myself, my way of thinking.

Give it to God. Pray for these ones that are so lost or maybe just living the lie of the world. God, you do control my life. Please help me guide these ones. I love them all.

I know it's your will. I understand they have to want it. Yes, I know you are fighting Satan for their soul now. I promise you I will never give up.

Now I understand what you meant by the devil will try all kinds of new things on me, anything to get me back. Some of the stuff hurts my heart very much. Then, I can feel you inside fixing me again. Thank you for all you do for me. I truly am one of your chosen. Yes, I know I'm blessed for the reminder of this human life.

I know it takes a very strong person to do what you had me do. This life you gave me is so amazing. I can't even try to explain the gifts you give. I pray people see the awesomeness of your love before it's too late. Thank you, God, again. I don't deserve what you do. Please help the ones in need. Love forever.

Yes, the devil speaks to us. His lies are so easy for me to see today. If we are not careful, he will act like God, trying to get us to do something his way. You see, this is just the beginning of it. When you do what he wants, he's sitting there rubbing his hands together, knowing that you're headed his way. Yes, he can and will deceive you. Remember, he is the king master of the lowest garage on earth.

Satan will do whatever it takes to get you in his grip. If you are new and trying to stay in your walk with Jesus, believe he is going to try even harder to get you. We all know he lies, telling you things like your not good enough or you will never be able to do that. He will tell you things like the ones trying to help you are just going to hurt you. You never could do that before, why do you think you can now.

Yes, Satan will twist things around in your head until you start thinking what is good is really bad. Just do it your way!!!

I'm telling you this, but you still let him get a hold of that string. He will keep pulling you closer and closer until he has a grip on you. Stand up. Ask Jesus to help. Learn the difference between the voices. Know that what is good or right is of God. If it's bad or hurts, then it's of the devil. Get it!!! God loves all.

Sometimes, we try to do what we want thinking it is what has to be done at that time when we are doing it for all the wrong reasons. We really don't think that far into it. It's like we have to prove something to ourselves. Then when we do this, it's all wrong. You get lost in the darkness wandering around in circles for hours.

What happens then, we get mad or disappointed, right. I have learned to stop and look at the big picture. Why is this happening to me? It's because God let me do it my way. See, I tried to take control. All that happens when I do what I want, I get lost in the dark.

See, I can still learn things. Stop trying to take control. When God has everything I need, when I do as he wants, my days are smooth and easy. Everything falls into place. Just trust his way always and believe.

I was praying last night for his guidance. Once again he pulled me from the darkness. This time it was from my own mind. Yes, that is where I was lost. Now, I can see where I listened to the wrong voice. I started thinking about what was going through my head.

It's amazing how God will be right by your side even when you are trying to put yourself above his guidance. I have learned to see the devil's lies. I just didn't think this one out, but I did learn fast that I was going down the wrong path.

Thank you, God, for your help and all you do for me. Once again, I'm on the path home.

It is not for us to judge anyone. We must be stronger than they are. For us, the children of God can see the devil's hand at work. Pray for the ones Satan has deceived for their hearts are closed. Their eyes do not see. They only understand the ways of the world. They may claim to be with God, but we can see. We know the devil has them. Satan is in their minds. They can not think God's way.

Their hearts, Satan holds so tight. It can not let God's love in, so pray for them that they might see God's light. Maybe then what they say just might turn into belief. Then and only then can they break the devil's grip.

Now those of you that think you are good with God, you believe that you can do anything you want. You believe that no matter what you do, you are safe, that God will never be disappointed in you. How do you think God feels when you purposely set out to hurt one of his children. You lie and deceive to get what you want.

Have you ever read the Bible? You know those things are sins, but you really don't care, do you. All that matters to you is to get what you want. For real, think about this. If someone did this to your children, how would you feel about it. My biggest question is your salvation. Do you really think God is ok with you doing this?

We know his children are priceless, so why would you try to hurt them. Just look at what he did to the angels that did wrong. As it says in 2 Peter 2:4 God did not spare angels when they sinned, but sent them to hell, putting them in chains of darkness to be held for judgment. Now look at yourself. Angels are above us, or do you believe that you are better than they are.

Do you think that you are like God. Now that you have been saved, you can do whatever you want to. Have you forgotten that you had to be washed by the blood of Jesus to be cleansed of all your sins, that Jesus said to go and sin no more. I bet you missed that part, "Sin no more".

How many times will Jesus have to bleed for you? How much of his blood has to be given for your sins? Living the way you are, you should be on your knees every night asking for forgiveness.

Did God not say it would be better not to have known the way of righteousness than to have known it and get caught up in the ways of the world, to turn your back on the sacred command that he has passed to you. I really don't know what goes through your head.

I do know God means everything to me. I will always follow his way. I could never set out to willfully hurt one of his children. God says to love others as yourself. Jesus says to love others as he loves you.

Where do you get that it's ok to bring false testimony on someone, to make up lies about them, to deceive others into believing what your saying. Have you not read Matthew 12:37.

For by your words you will be acquitted, and by your words you will be condemned.

So tell this grateful believer how big of a Christian you are again. Remember, God knows all, hears all, sees all. Are you truly 100% with God? Not if you do this stuff. You know even after all that you have done, I forgive you! Yes, I do.

I do because God has flooded me with his gifts of Grace, Mercy, wisdom, knowledge, forgiveness, redemption, freedom, happiness, joy and I can't forget the last one. The one gift above all his gifts, "His love". When you have his love in you, all things are different. You truly love all people, animals and all of nature. Your eyes will be opened to the lies of the world that tell you it's ok to hurt people.

How about this one. Look out for number one. To you I ask - who is number one, yourself? Think about that for a minute.

We all are children of God. It's our actions that make us look ugly. We as humans, hate, lie, cheat, steal, and judge others bringing false testimony on someone. All of this shows that you don't understand his words. To love God with all you are, to love others as you love yourself. Get it, you can't love if you don't love yourself.

God's love is an amazing place to live. It took me a lot of understanding to be able to fully get to this place. The reward is worth everything. You see, God has been showing me his love from day one. I keep trying to learn more and more.

It seems like every day he is showing me different parts. Some hurt my heart, some so joyful, I can't help but smile. The whole time I'm learning about it. Then, other times, it's hard to understand.

This is when God has to help me. Sometimes, he uses others to help me. These people mean so much to me because I can see his hand at work. It's so awesome to really be able to see how his love works in others. You see, God told me there are others that don't understand his love the way I do.

I have asked for something most don't. I asked to know all of God's love. Yes, there is good and bad, hurt and joy, happiness and sorrow. How can you really know love. If you don't understand all parts of it. I can truly tell you I know love like I never knew love before.

I have so much love for others. I can forgive others when they do wrong to me. This forgiveness comes from my heart. I can see how everything God does comes back to his love.

He shows me how some have been led astray, taught ways that God doesn't say, being taught wrong by false teachers. He does tell us about these ones in the Bible. God says to watch out for these people. They say they're of God, but teach the ways of the world.

They tell people that God values money, gold, silver and possessions. Say they are valued by what they own. That once they are saved they can do whatever they want. They can live the way of the world, put money and themselves before God. That as long as they come to church on Sunday, give the church their 10%, all is well with God.

I know that God can't mix with the ways of the world, so why would people believe this? They do because the one telling them this is a pastor or preacher. That tells me they can't be reading the Bible. If they would just open it and read, then they would understand God's way. Yes, I ask questions about what I read. I guess it's all about who you ask. Try asking God, Jesus and the Holy Spirit. This is where you will get the truth, the whole truth and nothing but the truth.

Stop thinking you can buy your way into heaven. Just because you pay your 10% doesn't mean you are going to heaven. Maybe you should try living God's way. All God wants is for you to give 100% of yourself to him, but I will tell you this. If you can't let go of money, you will never fully know his love.

I pray for you, and forgive you of what you have done. See, God does love you even if he doesn't like what you are doing. Me, I'm just a way for his love to enter this world. I pray one day you know what God's beautiful love can do. Understand there is no in-between. God is on the move. Life is going to hit you right in the face. There will be a lot of people in awe and disbelief.

Thank you God.

People will twist and distort all things. To get the outcome they want. Their way of thinking, their beliefs. They will actually try anything they can to have it their way. They really don't care who they hurt, just as long as they get what they want. That's it. It's all about them. Even when they claim to be children of God, they twist God's words to fit their hearts. What they want or believe.

God was right. They are the ones that get so caught up in the world. They actually believe that is how life should be, living the lie of the world the way the devil has made it. It's so easy for us humans to believe. Why, because we always want to take the easy way out. What we want or desire. We have learned to live for ourselves. Not to care about others.

When we do this, we are falling farther away from God. The life he made for us is so much better. When we honestly care about others, truthfully, this is what everyone needs in their heart. When I see people not caring, twisting facts around to fit what they want, that really hurts to know that people don't care. They only care about themselves.

Some just want to hurt others. They get joy or happiness from others hurt. This shows you even if they claim to be a child of God, the devil can still have a hold on them. Sometimes they upset us or bring anger to us. Please don't let the devil get in you. Keep God in your heart all the time. Never let your faith go. God told me to humble myself and pray for them. Early this morning I learned this. AMAZING!!!

This I have to ask. How many of you can walk away from everything you know. Your way of life, your family, all the people you know, start completely over, new life. Honestly tell me if you can even imagine the strength it would take just to change everything and everyone in your life, to start living a happy beautiful life full of joy, love, and forgiveness. Are you strong enough to do this for real.

Never say, "that's impossible". I've heard impossible is just a word for somebody that doesn't want to try. You see, I did just that. Yes, a complete change just to get myself on the road to God. I had to get away from all things. I couldn't carry others' burdens with me. They want to live in drama and lies, so I walked away from all. I did what had to be done.

You see, I had to carry my cross up the hill. I had to pour all my sins and burdens out at the foot of the cross, hand my life over to God. Jesus washed me clean with his blood, forgave me of all my sins. Yes, God took my life away. He gave me the miracle of new life, his life. God took me the lowest form of human garbage out of darkness.

Yes, I was living with Satan, doing everything he wanted me to do, so God poured his love in my heart, changed me into who I am. I'm not even close to the one I was. The people that know me from back then can see this. It's the ones that know but don't see. Or maybe they don't care to see. That really does hurt my heart.

I have learned with God's grace to accept how others feel even if it hurts, so I pray for them, love them, and yes, I forgive them too. Now, getting back to what I was saying.

When we can understand and believe, we actually receive God's love. Our heart changes then our thinking changes. We actually see things differently. It's so amazing how Jesus changed things. The world sent him to die on a cross. He loved us so much, he freely gave his life. What does that tell you? His love will change you if you open your heart.

Stop and take a really good look at what is happening in your life now. It's time to pick up your cross and make that journey up the hill. Lay your life down at the foot of the cross. A complete sacrifice. Don't hold on to anything. Experience the wonderful gifts of God. Jesus gave his life to give us a way to God. With this, we get God's grace, mercy, forgiveness, and freedom. There is no greater love! Amen.

Now, I'm seeing people judge themselves. Yes, we all know we are sinners. That doesn't stop us from putting ourselves down, saying we are the biggest let down, or that we are the worst of the worst. You see, we really are harder on ourselves than anyone could ever be then we get mad at others for what they say about us.

Now, if you understand this, tell me why others do a flip. They boast about themselves, keep telling others of what they do or how they are better than others in their eyes. Then, some of them want to show their power over others just because they might hold a higher rank or position.

I understand that we do have bosses, supervisors and managers. These positions have to be handled the right way, not showing others your power over them. If you put God in everything you do, then you will see what I'm saying. Stop patting yourself on the back. Start working with those under you. Help others out that need help or guidance.

Why treat people like they are garbage or a plague. Communication that is what is needed most. If we don't talk to others, how can we expect them to know what is wanted. Ok, now we get to this group. The people that think they are perfect, saying that they are equal to Jesus, that he is not their higher power, that nobody is above them not even God. In other words, saying they are God.

They say Jesus was just a man, no different than they are. They say Jesus did sin, but he used words to manipulate the law. Believe me, they are supposed to be christians. They go to a very big church and have these beliefs. It makes me wonder what is actually being taught to them.

Jesus did say there would be a lot of false teachers. When you hear this, do you wonder why? So many people want to know Jesus, and we have pastors or preachers teaching them wrong making them believe it's true. This is very heartbreaking for me. I know God, Jesus, and the Holy Spirit. Maybe not as good as some do. Then maybe more than some that have known him a lot longer than me.

God, Jesus, and the Holy Spirit will always be higher than us, so what about the ones that do in the name of God, but they do it their way. They say it's all about God just to many things wrong. This is how the world gets into what we do, making little changes until it's a big thing.

One thing that I don't agree with is separation. God says to treat all as yourself. Do you really understand this. Stop the separation of all men and women. I know people talk about me because I'm with women helping them out more than I do men. There are two reasons for this. First, God says we are his children. He doesn't say man is his children. That makes us equal.

My second reason is my past life. Don't get me wrong, my past is gone, but my conscious is still with me. I still remember how badly I treated women. Yes, I have been forgiven of my sins. We still remember what we did. We were weak or we tried to show power. We didn't care about others or ourselves. Now, we are strong with God and Jesus by our sides.

Now this brings me into my next thing. Some people won't like this. It won't be the first time. People say that recovery is hard that they struggled to keep clean only because they believe the lie, that it's a disease when we know it's a choice. Yes, you won't get any sympathy from me. I know I have lived that life. Stop crying and whining like the world owes you.

Grow up! I have had it with you going around saying it's a struggle everyday.

How can that be if you walk with God. God redeemed you. Do you know the meaning of redemption. Jesus's blood washes you clean. Do you understand that? There is only one reason it's a struggle. You still want to do it.

If you truly walk with God, all wants and desires are gone. Let me tell you all something. After I got high the first time, I was hooked. I started looking for the better high. I got high because I wanted to hear that it was my choice. Yes, I understand the sickness.

After you go through the withdrawals, you realize it's no worse than the flu. After you are off of it, there is no reason to use again. It's only if you want to. YOUR CHOICE. If you stay in your walk with God, completely devoted then you will never use again. THIS HAS TO BE YOUR CHOICE TOO!

Make your choice!

One day, all things will be revealed to you. That is the day that you will be in awe and disbelief. I have tried to help you but I can't do it for you. Open your eyes and your heart to God's way. Believe me, it is a lot easier if you have someone to help you.

Just imagine how it will feel when you see all the things you believed in become known to you for what they really are. The lies of the world, the hurt, disbelief, then the question why? Why was I raised believing this, why was I taught this? Then, you get the question, has the world really done this to us. The answer is yes and no.

See, the world has shown us this for a long time. We the people chose to live this way. So, now do you see. It was our choice too. Are you starting to understand the grip the enemy has on us? Satan has been here a lot longer than we have. He knows how to twist things around on us and get us to believe his lies, his way.

When this day comes when your eyes are opened, call me. I will help you find the right path. We all need a little guidance sometimes. I'm here to help you. Just hope I'm still here when you need me.

God bless you!!!

In closing, humans, were made for companionship. Without this, we are very lonely creatures who get into a lot of messed up things. God wants all to come together in unity. I see so much division in this world today. People are putting their opinions where it doesn't belong. If people would just back up and look God's way, you would see this world can be a lot better place.

We see this division even in churches. They are divided over people's opinions. Some over just the color of the carpet. Is that really a reason to leave a church? If we could just come together and understand God for who he is, that he wants us together in unity, the day the churches can come together is the day we overcome this world, but then we have people going on their opinion and sometimes their interpretation of what they read or believe.

They twist things around to be the way they think it should be. If only we all would get over ourselves and what we want to be right. We should start living God's word, what he says is right which is unity, togetherness, relationships, companionship, so are we prejudice.

Prejudice doesn't just mean color. When you start dividing people over your opinion or somebody else's opinion, it's called prejudice. Or you put people in age groups or divide men and women same thing. Doesn't God say he wants all to come to know him? He doesn't say he just wants all men to come to know him, so why do people try to divide. Yes, I hear you. It's the devil working in their head. Thank you God. You always answer me. I understand, it doesn't matter what people believe he will get in their heads, twist their understanding around till they start making things the way he wants them. Just like I see at some places they keep men away from women. If this is what God wanted, then he wouldn't have made Eve in the first place.

You see, God gave us togetherness, friendships, companionships, and relationships, so who are we to disrupt and alter what God has done. See what happens when you let the devil get in your head. You start believing the lies he tells. Really should look at everything God's way before making a decision. God only wants good for us, so stop trying to put yourself ahead or over God.

My prayer is that you overcome self and understand God's way. Amen.

Printed in the United States
By Bookmasters